CRITICAL CHAIN

Eliyahu M. Goldratt

THE NORTH RIVER PRESS

THE NORTH RIVER PRESS
PUBLISHING CORPORATION
P.O. BOX 567
GREAT BARRINGTON, MA 01230
(800) 486-2665

Manufactured in the United States of
America

ISBN 0-88427-153-6

CRITICAL
CHAIN

Chapter 1

"This board meeting is adjourned," announces Daniel Pullman, the domineering chairman and CEO of Genemodem. The elegant conference room hums with conversation as the directors start to depart. The last quarter was the best in the history of the company. The directors are pleased, but no one is overly excited. They have come to expect it. For the past six years, almost every quarter has been better than the preceding one.

"I want to have a word with you," Pullman tells Isaac Levy, smiling and continuing to shake the hands of the external board members. When everybody else leaves they sit down.

"Have you had a chance to read McAllen's final report?" Pullman asks.

It was Levy, the executive vice-president of engineering, who had insisted on hiring a consulting firm to do an in-depth analysis of Genemodem's product development. The analysis was not restricted just to engineering, it covered the entire process. Starting with examining the way they decide on the features of a new modem, through the development process, and of no less

1

importance, examining the way the new design is handed over to production and marketing.

Not that they had been complacent. Embarking on new technologies, new tools, even new management methods is the norm in their company. You cannot be among the leaders otherwise. Nevertheless, Levy insisted on bringing in experts from the outside. "There must be many things that we take for granted," he had claimed. "Things that only outsiders are able to see." Pullman supported him fully. Actually, no one really objected.

It was no small effort, and it did not come cheap, but at last, a week ago, they had received the four-hundred-page report.

"I really think they've done a very good job. There are many things they point out that we overlooked. We got our money's worth and then some," Levy says.

"Agreed. The report contains many good things. But I am concerned with what it does not contain. Isaac, if we were to implement everything they talk about, how much do you think our development time would shrink?"

"Hard to tell. Maybe five percent. Maybe not even that."

"That's my impression as well. So, we explored every conventional avenue and, as we expected, the answer is not there." Pullman stands up. "There is only one thing left to do. Isaac, launch the think tank."

"It's a long shot." Levy stands up as well.

"Very long, but we are skating on very thin ice." On his way out, Pullman adds, "We must find a way to rectify it. We must."

Isaac Levy looks at the three young managers sitting in front of his desk. He does not particularly like what he sees. They are not senior enough. All three are too young and too inexperienced for the task. But that was Pullman's decision.

"Isaac," he had said, "a senior person is already engraved with the way we are doing things. If there is someone who can find us a much better way, it's a young person. Young enough to be rebellious, young enough to be unsatisfied with our rules. Do you remember how young and inexperienced we were when we started? We broke every convention, and look at where we are now!"

Isaac didn't see any point in reminding him that they also "succeeded" in running their first company into the ground.

"Do you know each other?" he asks the three. "Why not introduce yourselves. Mark, you start."

"I'm Mark Kowalski. I'm with engineering."

Mark is thirty-two years old. A big man, with a voice to match. He has been with the company for eight years and recently was promoted to project leader of the A226 model. He is not the rebellious type that Pullman wanted, and Levy is not happy about risking the development of the A226, but they need a good group leader.

"Mark will be your group leader," Levy adds. "We think he is open enough to handle constructive criticism, knowledgeable and sensible enough to reject impractical criticism, and pleasant enough to ensure harmony. And if he is not, you tell me."

They are too nervous to laugh. This is the first time any of them has ever been invited to an Executive VP's office. Levy gestures to the woman to speak up.

She follows the pattern Mark used: "I'm Ruth Emerson. And I'm from marketing."

"And your job there?" Levy encourages her to elaborate.

"I'm a brand manager. I was on the team that planned the introduction of the A106."

The other two are impressed. The A106 is the current big success.

"Ruth was chosen," Levy explains, "because of her exceptional integrity. You are going to find out to what extent she is not afraid to ask questions."

"I'm Fred Romero." The last member of the group responds to Levy's look: "I'm a bean counter."

"Not exactly a bean counter," Levy laughs. "Fred is the rebel of finance. And at the same time the most respected project auditor that we have. You are all probably wondering why you are here?"

Mark and Ruth nod. Fred maintains his poker face.

"From now on, you are a think tank. Your mission is to find a solution to the biggest threat endangering the future of this company."

He pauses to look directly into the eyes of each one.

"Let me start by explaining the problem." Standing up, he grabs a marker and plots a curve on the white board. "Do you recognize this curve?"

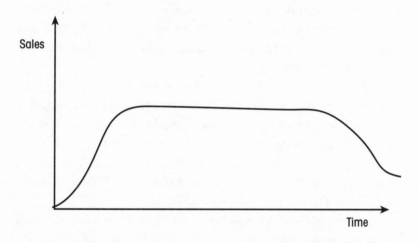

"You'll find it in every textbook. It's supposed to describe the lifetime of a product. First, sales are picking up as the product is introduced into the market, then they stabilize—it becomes a mature product, and finally, it fades out. Does it fit what we know about our products?"

They believe this is a rhetorical question until he says, "Well?"

"In our case, it looks more like a triangle," Mark volunteers. "Before we finish introducing a new modem into the market, we obsolete it by launching an even newer one."

"Which doesn't make sense?" Levy questions.

"I didn't say that," Mark hurries to clarify.

"If we don't launch the new modem," Ruth comes to his aid, "our competitors will. In any event, the current modem will be obsolete. The only difference is that we'll also lose market share."

"Correct. The frantic race in the market forces us to launch a new generation of modems every six months or so."

They all nod.

"Now let me explain something that you might be less familiar with. Our company's shares trade on Wall Street for sixty-two dollars and forty-eight cents, according to yesterday's paper. This high price is not justified by the company's assets, or even the company's profit. It is mainly based on the shareholders' expectations of future growth and future profits. Well-founded expectations based on our impressive track record. But do you realize how fragile that is?"

When no one answers, Levy continues. "To miss once, to launch an inferior product, or even to launch a good product three months after the competition, what will the impact be? Ruth?"

"It would be a disaster. We would lose significant market share."

"Where is good old-fashioned customer loyalty?" Levy sighs. "Gone." And then, in a more serious tone, "If we miss once, our per share value will plummet. The damage to the shareholders will be mammoth. If we miss twice in a row, maybe there won't be a company for us to work at."

He pauses. The three young managers look at each other.

"Our products have a very short life-span. Right now it's about six months, and all indications are that it will continue to shrink. At the same time, in spite of all our efforts, our product development time is roughly two years. Do you see our problem?" He pauses again.

After awhile he echoes their thoughts: "A development time of two years, when we have to launch the fruits of our development every six months, means only one thing. The question is not 'are we going to miss?' The question is 'when are we going to miss?' And remember, we cannot afford to miss even once."

They sit silently, digesting what has been said. Finally Levy speaks up. "Your mission is to find a way that will enable us to drastically cut our development time. For years we have been looking everywhere for the answer, and have not found it. You are what we have left. You are the ones who must find the answer."

"But, how?" Mark's face is red.

"That's the whole point, Mark. We don't know how! You'll have to tell us."

"What help can we expect?" he desperately asks.

"You will continue to be in charge of the A226. You will use that project as your test ground. You can choose anyone you like as your backup. Ruth and Fred, you are released now from all your other duties. If you need to visit other places, to attend conferences, or even to register for a formal Executive MBA program, just ask. No budget restrictions."

"To whom do we report?"

"Directly to me, and I do expect periodic progress reports."

"How much time do we have?"

"The A226 is scheduled to be ready in sixteen months. I expect it to be completed on or before time. By the way, think tank, if you come up with a good answer, there are a lot of shares waiting for you."

"How many are a lot?" Fred can't hold himself from asking.

"Ten thousand shares each," Levy answers. "Good luck."

After they leave, Mark says, "Good luck is appropriate. I guess we have about as much chance as winning the lottery."

"The reward is like the lottery, too," Ruth comments. "Ten thousand shares is a fortune. We are going to be millionaires."

"Fat chance."

Chapter 2

I pick up the memo and read it again, for the hundredth time.

Dear Rick,

You have been assigned to teach a course in the Executive MBA program.

We need to determine which course it will be.

Does Monday at 2 P.M. suit you?

Jim.

Only three sentences, but the implications . . . The implications . . .

I teach at a business school. But I am no longer at the bottom of the academic hierarchy. A year ago I was promoted from the doormat level of assistant professor to the semi-respectable position of associate professor. Frankly, it was a miracle, considering the abysmal number of academic papers I have had published. On the other hand, it wasn't, not if one takes into account the name I've built for myself as an exceptional teacher. It's no small effort turning each session into a learning experience, but it pays off; my courses are always the first ones to fill up.

Here, in black and white, is the latest proof. Just three sentences. This time I read the memo aloud.

"You have been assigned to teach a course in the Executive MBA program."

The words sound like a symphony. No wonder. Being assigned to teach in the Executive MBA program is a sure sign that next year I will be recommended for tenure. And tenure is Shangri-La. It's having a permanent position. Whatever you do, or don't do, you can't be gotten rid of. It's being in; it's security.

And security is what I need. And so does my wife. Like everybody else who wants a place in academia I was, listen to this, I was "accepted on probation." I think that only paroled criminals and young professors are formally on "probation." The difference is that professors are on probation for a longer period. Five years to prove myself as a good teacher. Five years to prove myself, to the other faculty members, as a team player.

"Does Monday at 2 P.M. suit you?"

Jim, buddy, it definitely suits me.

Two o'clock seems an eternity away. I decide to take a walk. It's cold outside. There's over a foot of new snow on the ground, but the sky is clear and the sun is high. It's almost one o'clock.

The first time I tried for tenure I blew it. Five years down the drain. It was a good university, bigger and more prestigious than this one. But I had to open my mouth. It's one thing to criticize the inadequacy of our textbooks, or to highlight that we are supposed to teach our students not just make them memorize. But it's a different ball game to criticize the publications of my fellow professors. Especially the senior ones.

They say that smart people learn from their mistakes while wise people learn from others' mistakes. Well, I'm not wise. I was never wise, but I am smart. All it takes is to be hit on the head, five to ten times, and I immediately learn my lesson. The details are ugly. It doesn't matter. What matters is that this time it's different. This time I'm making it. Big.

Almost nobody is outside. Or more accurately, no one except

for me is idly strolling. In spite of the patches of ice almost everyone is running. It's simply too windy. But I'm not cold.

Life is beautiful. I'm already an associate professor. Tenure is in the bag. The next step is getting full professorship, and then a chair. That's the ultimate. A chair means more time for research. It's being one of the big boys. It's a salary of over one hundred thousand dollars a year.

Such a salary is beyond my comprehension. Give me half of it and I'll be happy. After years of being a doctoral student living on a grant of twelve thousand a year, and too many years of living on the salary of an assistant professor . . . Hell, even a high school teacher seemed rich.

I rub my icy nose. I'll never get promoted to full professor if I keep neglecting the need to publish articles. One might get tenure by being a good teacher and a nice guy, but full professor is another story. "Publish or perish." That's the name of the game.

I hate this game. Maybe I hate it because I don't have the kind of ideas that can be converted into acceptable articles. I don't know how they do it. How they find those small examples that with enough mathematical modeling they can turn into another publication. I need something more tangible, more connected to the real world, real problems. Besides, now I am getting cold. I'd better head back.

I wonder what course Jim is planning to land on me. He wrote that we need to determine it, but it really doesn't matter. Whatever it is I'll have to spend a lot of time preparing. You can't compare teaching an Executive MBA course with teaching a regular MBA course, not to mention an undergraduate course. In the Executive MBA program the students are not full-time students. Actually, they are full-time managers spending one Saturday in class every two weeks.

My strides become longer. It's not just the flush of adrenaline, I'm half frozen. Teaching managers, that will be a new experience for me. They're not going to accept everything I say just because I'm quoting from a textbook. They will force me to deal with the real life situations they face. This may actually be a good thing. It might even give me some new ideas for research . . . and articles.

Ideas are not enough. I can't do research in a vacuum, at least not the type I'm willing to do. But maybe, if I play my cards right I can use these students as bridges to companies. It's possible.

I reach my building. A cup of hot chocolate will help me defrost. I stop near the machine; it's ten 'till two. I'd better hurry.

"Yes, thank you," I accept Jim's offer of coffee, and following his gesture, lower myself into one of his squeaky, uncomfortable upholstered chairs.

"Make it two," he says to Miriam, his colossal secretary, and chooses the sofa.

Status symbols are important in universities and Jim has a room that matches his position. A big room, a corner room. I should rephrase that. I don't know if status symbols are important in every university, but they sure are for the dean of our business school. Our dean will not let anyone forget which is the most important school. And he has a point. The business school has grown, by now, to over six thousand students—almost half the student population. Full professor Jim Wilson heads the most prestigious program of the school, the Executive MBA program. It's no wonder Jim was assigned such premises. I only wish he had better taste in furniture. On second thought, knowing the extent to which Jim is oblivious to anything materialistic, it's probably Miriam's choice. Yeah, that figures.

"Thank you for the opportunity," I earnestly say. "I will not let you down."

"I hope not," he smiles. And then, without a smile, "Richard, that's one of the things I wanted to discuss with you."

I lean forward. When Jim calls me Richard it is serious.

"Richard, as you know, there is no lack of more senior candidates who want to teach in the program. Do you know why I insisted on you?"

I don't. I only know that Jim liked me even before I was his doctoral student. I'll never forget that when I was struggling to get a second chance in academia he was the one who arranged for me to come here.

"I chose you because of your unique style of teaching," he surprises me.

"Teaching through open discussion?" I'm astonished.

"Yes," he says categorically. "For this program I'm more and more convinced that that is the only prudent way. The students have the relevant day-to-day experience. Open debate, steering a group of people to develop the know-how themselves, is how we should teach them. And I don't have many instructors who are both willing and know how to do it."

Now I understand, but it scares me. "Jim," I start to protest, "it's one thing to do it with regular students, but I'm not sure I can do it with actual managers."

"Why not? What's the difference?"

"What I'm actually afraid of is that I won't be able to steer them. That my theoretical knowledge will be insufficient relative to their practical knowledge," I answer frankly.

"Don't." Jim is firm.

"But . . ."

"Listen Rick. With these students, the most important thing is not to pretend to know when you don't. They pay a lot of money for tuition—much more than regular students, and they have an open door to the dean and even the president, and they don't tolerate garbage."

I start to wonder if I'm up to it. Maybe it will be my downfall.

My thoughts must be written all over my face because Jim starts to cheer me up. "How many years have we known each other? Huh? I know that I can trust you to be open with the students. And over and over you've proven to me that you know much more than you think you do. Don't be afraid to use your regular style. I'm sure it will work with them."

Not having much choice, I promise, "I'll do my best."

"Good." Jim is pleased. "Now all we have to do is decide

which course you'll teach." Heading toward the door he casually adds, "Have you given it a thought? Miriam, what happened to our coffee?"

He disappears into her room. A minute later he reappears with a tray.

"Jim, when I started my doctoral thesis, do you remember the warning you gave me?"

"I gave you so many," he grins, handing me a cup. "Which one are you alluding to?"

"Not to bite off too much," I remind him. "To forget the dreams about changing the world and take on a subject I could finish."

"Yes, I do. Good advice. Especially to a Ph.D. student."

I take a sip of coffee. "When is the right time to dream?" I ask.

He looks at me for a little while. "The middle age crisis!" he announces his diagnosis. "What does that have to do with which course you want to teach?"

I decide to answer his question with a question. "Isn't the course I'm going to teach in the Executive MBA program going to affect what research I'll be concentrating on?"

He thinks about it. "It might," he admits. When I don't reply, he grins, "So you want to make a difference. You want your research to be a yardstick for an entire field."

I nod.

He examines me for a little while longer. "I guess that the only way to flush it out of your system is to give it a try. So in which field do you contemplate making your contribution, Dr. Silver?"

"I don't know," I admit, ignoring the sarcasm. "A field in which the existing know-how is not enough."

"That's true for every field in business," he dryly says.

"What I mean is . . ." I'm searching for the words. "A field where it's apparent that the existing know-how is not giving satisfactory answers."

"What satisfactory answers are is a matter of opinion." Jim is thoughtful. "Try to specify what you don't want; maybe that will lead somewhere."

"I don't want to chase fads," I firmly say. "And I don't want a field that is overcrowded with research."

"That makes sense. Go on."

"I want a field that is in real need," I repeat myself. "A field in which no real progress has occurred for quite some time."

"Fine," he says, waiting for me to at last specify which course I do want to give. The problem is, I don't know. It's very embarrassing.

"Project management," Jim slowly says, "fits your description like a glove. If you are looking for a field in need, project management is a prime candidate. And in the last forty years or so, at least in my opinion, nothing new has been suggested."

"But, Jim, you teach that course."

"True, true." He starts talking to the ceiling. "And besides, I have used the course to start some interesting research. Quite interesting research."

"I could help you finish it. You know that I'm good at doing the library digging, and my writing abilities are decent."

"Yes, they are." He still stares upward.

"Jim, let me teach this course for one year. One year only. I'll do my best to help you finish your research. I'll do all the dirty work."

He shifts his eyes to the table and starts to talk, more to himself than to me. "I would like to concentrate on my production systems course. So much has happened in that field lately. It will be good preparation for a nice textbook." He looks me straight in the eyes. "So, about the project management course and the related research, what exactly do you suggest?"

Chapter 3

She is tall, over six feet tall. And slim. Elegantly dressed. Almost too elegant. Always. Not the type one calls beautiful, but striking. First impression is of expensive silk. Maybe because she never raises her voice, maybe because of the traces of a soft Southern accent. But it's just a first impression and it doesn't last for long. It's the underlying steel that is hard to escape noticing.

She is analytical, ambitious, an excellent manipulator, and she introduces herself as B.J. vonBraun. That's also the way her name appears on her letterhead. The rumor is that the first initial stands for Brunhilde. Nobody dares verify it. Her letterhead also says: University President. The crowned, unchallenged queen. And there is no king, not recently anyway.

It's summer, and Washington, D.C., is sweltering. It's hot even after sunset. But not at the restaurant where the university presidents are holding their formal dinner.

B.J. is seated between Bernard Goldsmith and Alistair Franklin. It wasn't too difficult to maneuver them to sit with her. Both are sharp, and experienced old acquaintances. But most importantly, they each have large business schools at their universities.

"How is your business school registration?" B.J. asks, as if just making conversation.

"Could be better," Alistair says casually.

Before B.J. has a chance to probe more deeply into this vague answer, Bernard does the job for her. "Do you mean that you've started to notice, as we have, that maybe the bonanza is about to be over?"

That's what she likes so much about Bernard; he always gets to the point without being aggressive. What she likes about Alistair is that he never avoids the issue.

"It's too early to tell," he answers. "But you may be right. This year we aren't going to send many 'we are sorry' letters."

Bernard nods. "It seems as if we are accepting anyone who knows how to spell his name. Hopefully. What about you, B.J.?"

Judging by his tone of voice, Bernard is as concerned about the subject as she is.

"The same, I'm afraid."

Mindlessly she continues to eat her Caesar salad. So it's not unique to her school. This is good news in a way, but alarming in another.

Alistair articulates what they are all thinking. "The last ten years or so were very good for us. Organizations' demand for new MBAs grew, and the desire of young people to acquire MBAs grew proportionately. We didn't have enough capacity to supply the demand. No wonder we enjoyed a hefty queue of applicants banging on our doors." He stops to sip his red wine. They wait for him to continue, but he doesn't.

Bernard picks up the ball. "So, is what we are witnessing now simply a result of the universities succeeding in building up enough capacity?"

"Probably." Alistair's eyes are fixed on his glass. "But it is not as simple as that. You know how systems tend to react. They almost always undershoot or overshoot. I'm afraid that the rapid decline in the number of surplus applicants indicates that we overshot."

"Judging by the rate at which business schools are still expanding all over the country, it's just a matter of time before we have empty seats," Bernard agrees with him.

Coming here was a good idea. B.J. is pleased. She is also pleased with the two partners she chose for dinner. "So we don't have enough applicants because the capacity of business schools has grown beyond the number of people who want to become managers?" she asks in her soft voice.

"Might be," Alistair succeeds in answering before the waiters start to serve the prime rib.

"This means that we had better restrain our business schools from continuing to grow at their current frantic pace. At least until we find ways to encourage more young people to choose management as a career path," Bernard thoughtfully concludes.

Alistair waits until the overly assertive waiter is satisfied before commenting, "It might be much worse."

"What do you mean?" asks Stanley from across the table. Apparently this conversation is of interest to other presidents as well.

"It might be that we don't have enough applicants because we are already over-supplying the market demand and the word is out that an MBA degree doesn't guarantee a lucrative job anymore."

"If that's the case," Bernard wonders aloud, "then it's not simply a matter of slowing the growth of our business schools. The challenge is how to smoothly shrink them. That's tough."

B.J. concentrates on the meat, evaluating what Bernard has just said. He is actually echoing her own concerns, but when she hears somebody else saying it she has her doubts. It can't be that bad. . . .

"On second thought," Bernard breaks into the silence, "we can boost the demand. All that's needed is to pass a law obliging every manager of a public company to hold an MBA. Make it statutory, like medical doctors or CPAs, or attorneys for that matter."

"Too much, too soon," Stanley objects. "I don't think that we should even think of legislation. It's against the essence of capitalism. And it's not practical, there is no way to enforce it. Besides, I don't think that the whole issue is relevant. Registrations for our school continued to grow this year, exceeding last year."

"I've talked with our friends at Harvard and MIT. They don't see any signs of softening either," Alistair contributes.

"They never do and never will," Bernard comments with a trace of envy. He picks at his prime rib and then pushes it slightly aside. "Their applicant list for everything is longer than my arm. What am I talking about, much longer than that. I've heard they can afford to accept only one applicant out of five. Considering the prices they charge, it's heresy."

"Why?" asks Jerry Preston. By now the individual discussions have died out. Everybody is waiting for Bernard to answer. He is not in a hurry, he likes being the center of attention. First he drinks a little red wine, then he dabs his lips with the white linen napkin.

"Do you want to know why? I can tell you why. Check their business school syllabus. They teach almost exactly the same material that we do. Maybe their professors are better researchers, but I doubt they are better teachers. The only difference between us and them is that graduating from one of the Ivy League schools is like having a license to steal. It's not any difference in substance, it's just the reputation."

"That's good enough," Stanley says flatly. "Besides, there is an important difference—they have better students. The best from all over the country apply to those schools, and as you said, they are able to pick just the *crème de la crème*."

"Once again, it boils down to reputation, not to substance." Bernard doesn't argue, he is just releasing some steam.

It might be that business schools are facing a crisis, B.J. thinks to herself. It might be that Stanley is right and the crisis is far on the horizon, but only the prestigious universities are immune. All the others are exposed.

"How do you build a reputation like that?" Jerry asks.

"Very simple," Bernard replies sarcastically. "You build the university two hundred years ago, and carefully cultivate the alumni." He looks around the table, challenging anyone to defy him. Stanley does.

"That's not the only way. We all know of cases where faculty have built national acclaim. They succeeded in gathering a group of exceptional scientists, whose breakthrough research put their department firmly on the map.

Alistair shakes his head in disagreement. B.J. knows exactly why. There is no way a small university like hers or Alistair's can attract people of such caliber. These exceptional people want, and are able, to go to the already acclaimed universities. Anyway, she simply can't afford the high salaries they command.

Maybe she can cultivate talent already existing in her business school? Support and encourage them in some way. . . . What way? And what is the likelihood that the business school has some unrecognized Feynman in their midst?

Chapter 4

I look around the class. There are many more students than I expected, almost thirty, but it doesn't matter; I've taught classes four times as large and I'm well prepared. I slaved all summer, reading everything I could lay my hands on. I interviewed over a dozen people with a lot of experience in project management, much more experience than these young managers have. I think I can handle anything they throw at me. Or at least I can swing at it.

They all take their seats. It's quiet. I'd better start.

As usual, the first row is almost empty. The last person to become quiet is sitting in the back row. Good. He is a large man, about my age. He can stand some abuse. "What's your name?" I ask, pointing at him.

I picked right because he doesn't try to pretend I am pointing at somebody else. "Mark Kowalski," he replies in a booming voice.

"Why have you chosen this course?" I ask bluntly. One thing is for sure, I have everybody's attention. They are not accustomed to my teaching style. A professor is supposed to lecture, not interview. Half are looking at me, half are looking at him. Some are smiling.

"I'm a project leader," he answers.

When I don't reply, he continues. "I work in a company that produces modems. I'm in charge of one of the development teams."

I continue to stare at him, but he doesn't add anything more. The situation becomes really uncomfortable when I finally say, "You haven't answered my question."

I look around. Nobody meets my eye. Nobody wants to be the next victim. I return to Mark. "Do you have any problems managing your project?"

"Not really," he answers.

"So why have you chosen this project management course?"

He starts to grin. "I guess I do have some problems," he admits.

"Can you elaborate?"

"Well, I didn't start this project, and the person before me made some wild promises that, I'm afraid, are unrealistic."

"Like?" I press him.

"Like the expected performance of our new modem and the time it will take to deliver it."

Some other students are grinning with empathy.

"And you expect," I look him straight in the eye, "that what you are going to learn in this course will enable you to perform some miracles?"

"I wish," he uncomfortably admits.

"So, why have you chosen this course?" I repeat my question.

"Look," he says. "I am a project manager. I am working toward my MBA. This is a project management course, isn't it?"

"Ah! So you chose the course because its title resembles your job title?"

He doesn't answer. What can he say? It's time to let him off the hook.

"Can anybody tell me why he or she chose this course?" I ask the class.

Nobody answers. Maybe I was too intimidating.

"When I was a student," I tell them, "I chose courses that were given by professors who were known to be light on homework. I'm afraid that I'm not one of them."

It helps a little, but not much.

"Listen," I continue. "We all know that you are here to get the degree. To get a piece of paper that will help you climb the organizational ladder. But I hope that you want something more than that. That you want to get know-how that can really help you do your job."

Heads nod around the room.

"You have to choose between two alternatives. One is that I'll stand here, on the podium, and lecture for the entire semester. I can flabbergast you with optimization techniques and take you through every complicated heuristic algorithm. It will be tough to understand, even tougher to use and, I guarantee you, won't help you one iota.

"Or, we can put our heads together and, drawing from your experience and the know-how that exists in books and articles, we can try to figure out how to manage projects better. Which do you choose?"

Not much of a choice is it?

At the back, Mark raises his hand. "So what should I expect from this course?"

Good question. Good man. "Mark, you told us you have problems with your project. I think that this course should give you better ability to deal with those problems."

"Fine with me," he says.

Turning to the class, I start. "Assume that I have good knowledge of the know-how as it is written in books and articles. What we have to find out now is the level of experience you have with projects. So, besides Mark, who else is deeply involved in projects?"

A slim redheaded young man in the third row raises his hand. "My name is Ted and I work in a construction company. Everything we do is a project."

"How long have you been working there?" I ask.

"Six years."

"Excellent," I say. "Anybody else?"

To my surprise, nobody else raises a hand. I'm saved by a blond woman, sitting by herself in the front row. Hesitantly, she asks, "Can you define what you mean by a project?"

I swiftly scan in my mind four definitions I read in textbooks. Somehow they all seem too pompous to me. How can one relate to a definition like "A set of activities aimed to achieve a specific objective and have a clear start, middle and end." If I want to bring this course down to earth and relate it to their situations, I'd better not quote any of these oversimplified or complicated definitions. Rather than defining, I choose to describe. I say, "In your work, have you come across a complex initiative that in order to manage it, people have to draw the picture of what they are supposed to do?"

"I don't understand," she replies.

"Some block diagram of the various steps that must be accomplished in order to achieve the objective, showing which steps should be done in sequence and which in parallel. Or alternatively, some time charts, which display when each step should start and when it will end. If you came across a situation where people use such charts, you came across a project."

"I see," she says.

"Are you involved in projects?" I ask her.

"According to your definition, I am," she answers. "I am a brand manager, and we spend a lot of time building such charts before we launch a new product."

"And your name is?"

"Ruth Emerson."

Her example probably helps the others because it quickly becomes apparent that everybody is involved with some type of project. Some of them are working in an almost pure project environment, like Mark in design engineering, redheaded Ted in construction or Charlie, in the Hawaiian shirt, who told us he is in software programming.

Others are interacting with, or even conducting projects. Like Ruth in marketing; Fred, an accountant who also audited some projects, and Brian, who is involved in the expansion of his plant. What is very good is that between them they cover a broad spectrum of project environments. But that is also dangerous. If I do not succeed in steering them to concentrate on what is common to all their projects, we are bound to flounder all over the map.

That is why I don't inquire about their specific projects. Rather, I ask, "The channel tunnel, what do you know about it?"

Ted, my redheaded student, is the first to comment. "Isn't it the train tunnel between England and France?" When I confirm, he continues, "I read that they have huge budget overruns."

"In the billions," Fred, our accountant, adds.

"It became such a big problem," Ted is on a roll, "that at one point they contemplated stripping some of the ambitious original design."

To encourage more conversation I ask the class, "What else?"

Ruth, in the front row, picks up the ball. "I saw the grand opening of those tunnels on TV. The queen herself christened it. The opening was a few months late and they were still unable to run trains."

"A classic example," I summarize, "of a project that didn't finish on time or on budget."

I give them another famous example; the oil rig platforms in the North Sea. These oil rigs are enormous plants built three hundred meters above the floor of one of the most stormy oceans in the world. From each platform they drill not one, but many, oil wells. They drill at angles of up to 57 degrees to hit oil three kilometers below the surface. Then they have to separate the oil from the sand before pumping it through pipes to shore. No wonder the investment in each one of those huge projects is close to four billion dollars. One might think that after putting up several of these big babies they would have their act together. It's not the case. It's been said that they plan a project meticulously, then multiply by four and pray.

"Well," I tell the class, "prayers are clearly insufficient. In the early nineties the top gun of StatOil, the Norwegian oil company, was forced to resign due to mammoth overruns on one of these projects.

"You see, Mark," I jokingly add, "you are not the only one whose project does not meet its due date. At least in your case, you are not going to run over budget."

"Yes, I will," he calls out, and then explains. "The project manager before me, the one who so carelessly spread promises, is now my boss. He is determined to save face, so he has forced me to take on more people and use expensive subcontractors. We definitely are going to be over budget, the only question is by how much."

"There is another question. Who is going to be blamed for it?" I add.

"Not him, I'm afraid. Knowing my boss, I'm definitely the one going to be blamed."

"So what are you going to do?" Charlie, our software manager, is sincerely concerned.

"Nothing," Mark brushes it off. "In engineering, every project is overrun and overdue. Besides, there is another tack. When push comes to shove, we will reduce the targeted specifications of the project."

To stress this last but important point, I ask, "Do you do it frequently?"

"More than we like to admit," he answers.

"Has anybody else come across a project that due to its overruns and its being overdue, compromised on its original specifications?"

"I don't know if you can call it compromising the original specifications," Brian comments, "but when they finished our new offices, only four months after they were due, we moved in only to find out we didn't have desks, and the air conditioning was not yet functioning."

Before I have a chance to comment, Charlie confidently states, "Everybody knows that projects don't finish on time or on budget, and if they do it means they had to compromise on content. Especially in systems programming or product design."

"That is not necessarily the case," I say. "Occasionally, there are design engineering projects that finish much ahead of time, significantly under budget and deliver more than was promised."

Those with any experience working in or with design engineers, which means about half the class, find it hard to believe such a claim.

"In the early fifties," I continue, "the Russians announced that they, too, had an atom bomb. That came as a total surprise. It became apparent to the U.S. that it had to find a way to monitor what the Russians were doing in their vast Asian territories."

"That's how the space satellite program started," one of the students guesses.

"I'm afraid that at that time satellites were to be found only in science fiction books," I have to disappoint him. "But, jet airplane technology was rapidly developing. One reputable engineer, Clarence "Kelly" L. Johnson, suggested building a plane that could fly at altitudes above the ceiling reached by fighter planes. Do you know how much time it takes to develop a new airplane? I mean from concept to an operational weapons system?"

"Over ten years," Brian says confidently. "I served in the Air Force."

"That's doesn't make you an expert, yet," Ted picks on him.

"Usually, it does take more than ten years," I confirm Brian's answer. "The U-2 was developed in a surprisingly short time. Eight months after start, this airplane was already flying over Russia, taking pictures."

"Until 1960, when Francis Gary Powers was shot down," Brian demonstrates that he does know the details.

Everybody is impressed. Slightly with Brian, mainly with the achievement of the people who built the U-2. The only one who looks skeptical is Fred. The accountant.

I look at him, raising one eyebrow. That's enough to make him start.

"You gave us two examples of major snafus, Professor Silver. Can you give us more?"

"No problem," I smile broadly, "how many would you like?"

"You also gave us one example of a major success. Can you give us more of those?"

"I'm afraid not," I admit, slightly embarrassed.

"Exactly as I suspected," Fred responds flatly.

Dear Fred has given me an excellent opportunity to drive home the conclusion I wanted them to reach, but I cannot control myself from asking, "Why did you have this suspicion?"

"From experience." And then he elaborates, "I have worked as a financial manager in three large companies. I have audited more new product development than I care to remember. And like every project auditor, I am quite cynical. Not that I haven't seen projects that do finish within the original, allotted budget, but they are the exceptions."

"That is probably the situation in design engineering," I confirm. "Charlie, is it much different in computer programming?"

"In computer programming we say that a project will always run out of time but never run out of excuses."

I join the laughter. When it dies down, Brian comments, "In the Air Force we always met the final due date." After three seconds he adds, "That means that we didn't meet the first due date that was set for the project, or the second one."

When I can finally speak again, I point at Ted, "What is the situation in the construction industry? Over there, there is less uncertainty regarding the content of the project."

"That's correct," he says. "Our projects are usually not so different from each other so we have a lot of experience." And grinning, he adds, "We also have a lot of experience using any change requested by the client to cover our butts for cost or time overruns."

I glance at my watch. It's time to start summarizing.

"Can we conclude," I ask the class, "that the problems common to all projects are," and turning to the board I write as I continue to talk, "the high probability of, 1. Budget overruns; 2. Time overruns; and many times, 3. Compromising the content."

Wall to wall consensus.

"We tend to blame it, in each specific project, on one string of bad luck or another. In my eyes, the U-2 project is important because it's different. It's unlikely that they succeeded in finishing in less than one-tenth the time just because of a streak of good luck. It must be that somehow they succeeded in avoiding the generic pitfalls that get almost every other project."

"How did they do it?" Ruth asks the question that bothers everybody.

"Wouldn't it be nice if we deciphered it?" I answer. "Which brings me to your assignment for the next class."

No matter what the age of the students, the reaction is always the same—a deep sigh.

Heartlessly I continue. "Select a project in your company. A project that has recently finished or is about to be finished. Interview the person running this project—the project leader. Interview the people who did the actual work, and interview the bosses of the project leader. Prepare two lists for class. One: the official reasons for the overruns. The second: the unofficial reasons.

"See you in two weeks."

I stop on my way home from the university to pick up some fried chicken. Judith is in New York for the weekend, so nobody is expecting me at home. I hope she enjoys her trip. On second thought, knowing too well what she enjoys most, I hope not.

Judith finds joy in buying things, currently, for our new house. Not exactly ours. We borrowed the money for the down payment. And the mortgage payments swallow my salary increase and then some. This summer I didn't make much extra by tutoring. It's tough.

But the house was such a sweet deal. A real bargain. Judith knows a bargain when she sees one, especially in houses. She is a real estate agent. This year she closed three deals. All involving other agents, so her share was abysmal. The last one she closed last week. Six hundred and eighty-seven dollars. That's why she is now in New York.

The flight and the hotel are about six hundred. Not a chance she will spend only eighty-seven dollars, and our credit lines are stretched to the limit. Maybe we should have another little talk? I shiver. Better not.

Chapter 5

B.J. looks out her office window. The campus is particularly beautiful at this time of year, when the trees are so colorful and the students, once again, fill the university with young life.

Less than a hundred yards away is the main entrance to the impressive complex of the business school. She watches Dean Page hurrying down the broad steps. He's heading straight to her office. It's not going to be a pleasant conversation.

B.J. pours the tea, and using silver tongs she neatly transfers two lumps of sugar and hands the cup to her guest. She doesn't need to ask, she knows what he likes; she knows him inside out. She has to. He is a very important player in her game.

"I'm sure you liked it," he gestures toward the general direction of her mammoth mahogany desk. He doesn't mean the desk. He's alluding to his thick, bound document, now resting there.

"For the most part," she smiles.

He is slightly older than she is, and dressed as elegantly. A few years ago his dress code was quite different; sneakers, open-necked shirts, nylon Windbreakers, a professor who liked to

29

blend into the academic environment. No more. Not since he reached the position he always wanted. He won by a narrow margin, but now his position is secure. The business school is his fortress. Professor Christopher Page II intends to stay the maximum term as dean. Maybe even to change the rules that define that maximum.

It's their informal meeting to discuss the business school's proposed budget for next year. They both prefer to hammer out their differences in private much before the budget is formally due. Not that Christopher Page is expecting any difficulties. His proposed budget is what B.J. would expect. The same fifteen percent or so increase from year to year, no surprises. Of course, they'll have to go through the ritual; she will ask for a cut, he will resist, in the end they'll compromise. He even knows on which items. He suspects B.J. knows as well.

"Let me tell you a story," B.J. softly says. "My first job was in a small private university in the Midwest. It was not always a small university. As a matter of fact, about twenty years before my time, it was quite large. Do you know what happened there?"

"No idea," he answers, wondering how she is going to tie it to a demand to cut his budget.

"They had a flourishing agricultural school," she continues in her soft voice. "They allowed it to grow about ten percent a year. It grew and grew, and with it, using your terms, the fixed assets grew: the number of classrooms, number of laboratories, number of tenured professors."

"And then . . ." Page says out of politeness.

"And then, agriculture did not need so many graduates any-more. Naturally, registration of new students dropped and fewer were eager to continue on to higher degrees. But the burden to maintain the buildings remained, and the need to pay the salaries of professors with tenure remained."

"It happens," he calmly comments, "in agriculture."

B.J. doesn't allow his comment to distract her. She hasn't yet finished her story. "The impact was not restricted to the agricultural school alone," she clarifies. "The financial burden was high enough to mandate a drastic cut throughout all the other schools. Some say it was a miracle that the university was not bankrupt."

She pauses. He doesn't comment.

"You don't think that it can happen to us?" B.J. inquires.

"Definitely not," Page dismisses the idea.

"Why?"

"One cannot compare agriculture to business," he says conversationally. "You don't need a university degree to succeed in agriculture. In that field there is no external pressure that forces people to go through higher education."

"And in business there is," B.J. encourages him.

"Without a doubt. Today, if you want to climb the corporate ladder you must have an MBA."

"Good for us," B.J. agrees.

Page is a little disappointed. He expected more decisive arguments from B.J. That's not the way to alarm him enough to voluntarily cut his budget.

"Chris," she continues, "there is another field that forces people to go through higher education. Lawyers must graduate from a university. Moreover, in law it's not an option, in business it still is."

Never underestimate her, he reminds himself, and aloud, he says, "I don't see the relevancy."

"I spoke with Paul Dimmers yesterday. You know him?"

"Quite well." Page is starting to dislike the direction their conversation is taking.

"They are facing a real problem, he told me. New student enrollments at their law school are less than half compared to three years ago."

Christopher Page examines her face. He cannot decipher anything. Impossible to figure out. Is she aiming at next year's budget, or at something much larger? There weren't any warnings. Maybe this is B.J.'s way of warning him? He decides to stop brushing it aside. At least until he can find out where B.J. really stands.

"How does Paul explain the drop," he inquires noncommittally.

"That's the interesting part," she answers. "It looks like they were talking about it for quite some time. If we had a law school in our university, no doubt we too would have heard about it before."

Page barely stops himself from saying, "Well?"

"Being a lawyer became a real fad," she starts to explain. "No wonder, considering the base salaries that were being offered. There was a flood of young people wanting to be lawyers. The schools ballooned. Almost a replica of the story I told you about my old university."

Page doesn't have any difficulty seeing how she intends to build the parallels to his business school. It's much more serious than he thought. She's not aiming at the present, she's questioning the foundation upon which his long-term strategy is built.

"You can figure out the story from there," she says. Nevertheless she continues; it's clearly important to her that it be verbalized. "Those many new students, after a few years, turned into many new graduates. So many that they outstripped the demand."

Page now has had enough time to figure out his response. First he must demonstrate to B.J. that he does understand her concerns, and then he must convince her to drop them.

So, without hesitation, he says, "Not all new law graduates could find a decent job. The word started to spread around and the number of applications of new students dropped."

"Quite so," B.J. agrees.

"Nothing to worry about," Page says in his most authoritative voice. He lays down what he considers his trump card. "We are far from saturating the demand for new MBAs."

It doesn't work. B.J. is not impressed. "Isn't the growth in enrollment at our business school the smallest it has been in years?"

"A temporary phenomenon," he dismisses it. "Nothing to worry about."

"Maybe," she says thoughtfully. "Maybe not."

Page cannot afford to leave it like this. "B.J., how can I put your mind at rest about this?" He signals that he is ready for business.

"I'm not concerned with the immediate future," she responds. "My nightmare is to be stuck with an expensive burden that will be almost impossible to trim. For example, you are budgeting for tenure for eight more professors. If push comes to shove such decisions may kill us. What about putting a freeze on all tenure, at least until the situation becomes clearer?"

"No, B.J., that would be a mistake. We need these people. If we don't give them tenure now, we have to let them go. Think of the implications. Think of the shock wave it would send. I understand your concerns, but, in my opinion, there is no reason for alarm. Definitely no reason for such drastic actions."

"Delivering some message is appropriate," she insists.

He knew that eight new tenure appointments would not fly. It was worth a try. "Maybe you are right," he smoothly bargains. "Maybe we should send a signal. The departments should not take us both for granted."

She waits for his proposal.

"I guess we could accept only six," he offers.

To his surprise she is not willing to counter-offer his number. "I'm still worried that what is happening in law schools can happen in business schools," she insists. "What are you suggesting we do about the possibility of a change in the trend?"

Page tries his usual tactic. "I'm not suggesting we dismiss it," he comforts her. "Not at all. We should think about it. Examine the probabilities. Do some research."

"Exactly right," she sails along. "Do we agree that the first, decisive indications will appear as the ability of graduates to get jobs?"

"I guess so," Page answers coldly, thinking about this new angle.

"Do we have to wait until it will not be easy for MBA graduates to get a job that matches their initial expectations?"

"When that happens I agree that the alarm bells should go off. But we are so far from it. Actually, I wonder if such a time will ever come."

Her way of arguing is to say, "Don't you think that as the two people with the responsibility we should monitor the situation?"

"Good idea." He starts to see how he can drag the issue to a committee, where it can be buried for good. "How do you suggest monitoring it?"

"Three years ago the school of business made a broad-scale survey among our graduates. They used the results as a promotional tool to encourage more enrollment."

"I initiated it," he says proudly. "It worked very well. And I do agree with you, we have to repeat the survey. Every year. That will enable us to hold our hand on the pulse of things. I'll initiate a committee to handle it. Right away."

She gently smiles at him. He tries hard to maintain his "collaborative" expression.

"We don't have time for committees, Chris." Before he can object, she turns around and walks to her desk. "Here are the results of our new survey. I think you'll find it interesting. Even quite alarming. But once you study it, I'm sure you'll agree with me that we have to put a total freeze on granting more tenure."

"First I'll read it, then I need time to evaluate, then we'll talk." Page tries to get back his balance.

"We definitely will. More tea, Christopher?"

Chapter 6

I enter the classroom. It's still noisy, not all the students are sitting yet, but on my table there is a pile of papers. I arrange them into a neat stack, and skimming through them, pick the one that looks the most professionally organized. "Fred Romero," I read aloud the authors name. The class quiets down.

I keep on reading, "Project title: New production facility in Malaysia."

"May I say something?" Fred asks.

"Certainly."

"This Malaysian project is not one that I'm involved with. I deliberately chose this project because for the projects I'm involved with, I already have some strong opinions about why things are the way they are."

"And you want to present an objective evaluation. Good thinking." And I continue to read from his report, "Project status: the Malaysian plant should have been fully operational eight months ago. Currently machines are installed in all departments except for one, but only three lines out of five are already operating. Output of the plant is currently less than thirty percent of target. Anything to add, Fred?"

"Only that I've heard some complaints that the quality is not up to par. But since I couldn't get any official numbers, I didn't include it."

"Fine. Next item on Fred's report is: Financial status. I love the way you arranged it."

"Standard procedure." He plays it down, but it's apparent that he enjoys the compliment.

"Financial status," I read again. "Due to budget overruns of sixteen point two percent and delays in production, the original estimate of three-year's payback is now modified to five."

"Does everybody understand the term 'payback'?"

Ruth probably knows the term. Nobody admits that he doesn't. Nevertheless, I explain. "Payback is the time period from investing until we expect the fruits of our investment to cover the investment. For example, suppose that you invest one hundred dollars and you get fifty dollars each year. Assuming no inflation, your payback period is two years. In Fred's case the calculations are a little bit more involved since the money is invested over a period of time. For investing in a new plant, payback of three years is considered to be a very good investment. Considering the risks, five is marginal."

"Five years is the current official estimate, but in my friend's opinion it's much too optimistic," Fred comments. "They are pushing for a formal estimate of a minimum of seven years, but since this project is the personal initiative of the CEO, I'm afraid that it will be some time before the estimate is corrected."

Fred's comments certainly help to bring his report to life. "Official explanation," I read, only to be immediately interrupted by Fred.

"Of course, I didn't interview the CEO. So what I'm calling here the official explanation I took from a memo outlining the explanations given to the Wall Street analysts."

"Even better," I say, and continue, "One: Particularly bad weather conditions that delayed construction. Two: Unforeseeable difficulties experienced by the vendors who supply the machines. Three: Longer than expected negotiations with the Malaysian government concerning employment terms."

I cannot stop myself from commenting, "There is something common to all of them. Do you see it?"

Ted is the first one to jump. "It's all somebody else's fault. The weather, the vendors, the Malaysian government."

"What did you expect?" Fred is slightly impatient. "That's corporate mentality; always blame the external world. But look at what I wrote under unofficial reasons. Here you will find finger pointing at functions inside the company.

"By the way, Professor Silver, I couldn't interview the current project leader, he is in Malaysia, but I don't think it matters too much since once the emphasis shifted from constructing the plant to running it, the project leader changed. I did interview the previous project leader and some of his people. Most of them are back at headquarters."

"Unofficial reasons given by the project leader," I read. "One: Corporate forced an unrealistic schedule to start with. Two: It was dictated that we choose the cheaper vendors, even though it was known that they are less reliable. Three: In spite of repeated warnings, efforts to recruit and train plant personnel and workers started too late."

"By the way," Fred adds, "on this last point, some other people told me that efforts to recruit personnel were late because the machines were late, and they thought it wasn't prudent to hire people and pay their salaries for nothing."

I thank him and continue. "Additional unofficial reasons, given by people reporting to the project leader. One: Too much reliance on vendor progress reports that in subsequent visits turned out to be less than accurate." I look at Fred for an explanation.

"Oh, there are many stories about vendors reporting progress on building our machines that later, on-site inspections showed they had barely started. Or, for example, in one extreme case, a vendor received a hefty order from another company and practically put our order aside for almost three months."

"I see," I say, and continue. "Two: Too loose supervision of the Malaysian construction contractors. Three: The overworked project staff were moved too frequently from one emergency to another. Four: Too many wasteful 'synchronization' meetings interrupted the actual work."

"Does anybody have a problem understanding the last two reasons?" Fred asks the class.

"No," comes the answer from all directions.

"Can you relate to all the items in Fred's report?" I ask.

And getting a positive response, I continue, "So let's try to use this report to come up with some general observations about projects. Who will offer the first one?"

"I already did," Ted says. "All the explanations for all the problems have one thing in common. It's somebody else's fault. All that we've heard is just a long list of finger pointing.

"We heard more than that," Mark comments in his booming voice. "There is a pattern here. The lower the level of the person, the more the finger points internally, rather than externally. You'll find the same thing in my report."

"Does anybody else see the same pattern in their reports?" I ask the class.

When almost everybody does, I continue to ask, "Which reasons should we consider? The ones offered by top managers who see the global picture or the ones offered by the lower level managers who are much more familiar with the actual details?"

The following discussion doesn't lead us anywhere. We start to flounder. Until Ted says, "One thing's for sure, we can't ignore the lower level managers' explanations. And if so, at least a major part of the blame is internal."

When we all agree, he continues, "It means that the company could have managed the project better."

"How?" Ruth is not too shy to ask.

"What do you mean, how?" Charlie is irritated by her question. "Look at what they are complaining about and fix it."

"I'm looking, and I still don't know how," Ruth answers calmly.

I look again at the list of reasons supplied by the people reporting to the project leader. Ruth is surprisingly observant. I start to realize that her "innocent" questions all stem from a rare ability to look at reality as it is. Since the class is not holding Fred's report, I explain Ruth's remark.

"These people complain about lack of sufficient supervision of the vendors, but at the same time they also complain that they are so overloaded they barely have time to deal with fires."

Ted doesn't give up on his opinion. "It just means that the company has to add more people to supervise the project."

"More people means more time and effort for synchronization," I point out. "Doubling the number of people four-folds the synchronization efforts. You probably noticed that these same people are already complaining that too much time is devoted to synchronization."

"They just have to find a better way to manage themselves," Ted concludes.

"How?" Ruth nails him.

"That's what we are here to learn," Ted passes the ball into my court.

"Thank you, Ted. So, from the reasons given by the lower level managers we can conclude that we have to find a better way to manage a project. No doubt. But what about the reasons given by top management. We can't ignore those reasons."

Agreed.

From the back row, "Can you please repeat the CEO's explanations?"

"Certainly. One: Particularly bad weather. Two: Unforesee-

able difficulties at the vendors. Three: Longer than expected negotiations with the Malaysian government. Can you see a pattern here?"

"Yes," Ted is once again the first to answer. "Blame it all on
uncertainty."

"Explain."

"Particularly bad weather," he quotes, "unforeseeable difficulties, longer than expected. . . . They are all expressions of
uncertainty; of the things that are hard to estimate at the start of
a project."

"And you think that there is nothing to it?"

"Not at all," he backs up. "Uncertainty is what typifies projects. It's the nature of the beast."

"If that's the case," I point out, "if that's actually the nature of
the beast, then we should find uncertainty underlying the reasons of everybody involved in the project, not just the top managers."

"We do," Ruth quietly says.

We go over Fred's list again. She is right. The project leader's
complaints all revolve around the uncertainty. He complains
about an unrealistic schedule to start with, unrealistic compared
to his estimations of the uncertainties. The vendors were chosen
according to cost and not according to their reliability, or in
other words not according to their ability to cope with uncertainties. And because of the uncertainty of the date at which the
plant equipment would be available, recruitment had to be delayed.

We move to analyzing the complaints of the people reporting
to the project leader. The vendors' issue. Surprisingly, initially
the class reacted as if it had nothing to do with uncertainties.
It took some time to agree that the vendors didn't want to deliberately sabotage the project (a major portion of their pay
was pending completion of their job). Why were they delayed?
For the same reason Fred's company was; they also suffered
from uncertainties. Then we agreed that most fires were a

direct or indirect result of uncertainties, and the constant efforts to re-synchronize stemmed from the fires and the ensuing delays.

"Let me summarize," I say. "We observed that fingers are also pointed internally. We agreed that this finger pointing does have merit, and we concluded that the company can do something about it.

"Then we examined the details and reached the conclusion that the thing to do is to better manage the project.

"What we now are saying is that the uncertainties embedded in the projects are the major causes of what we called mismanagement."

"So there's nothing anybody can do," is Charlie's conclusion. "You cannot force certainty on a situation that contains major uncertainties."

These same thoughts haunted me all summer. Is the lousy performance that we witness in most projects a *force-majeure?* A result of the embedded uncertainty? Or is there something that we can do?

At first it seemed like a stone wall. I would probably have given up, if it weren't for the U-2 example.

I start to steer the class toward the crack Jim showed me.

"Everybody in projects knows that projects involve a high degree of uncertainty. We are not the first ones to conclude it," I remind them. "Why isn't the uncertainty properly factored into the original estimation?"

"Because we cannot," Mark booms.

"What do you mean?" I ask. "Who prevents us?"

"Top management," he answers, and then elaborates, "take my project, for example. It was originally estimated to be completed in thirty months. But top management said that was unacceptable and trimmed all the safety. My boss agreed to try and do it in less than two years, which is an impossibility."

"So, you wanted thirty months and top management forced it

down to twenty-four months. The difference is twenty percent. Mark, do you really believe, considering the magnitude of uncertainty in product development, that twenty percent safety is enough?"

"It isn't, but what can we do? Top management doesn't allow us even that."

"I don't think so, but maybe our disagreement stems from the fact that we are talking about two different things. You are talking about the safety added to the project as a whole. I am talking about the safety added to each and every step in the project."

Judging by the students' expressions, I'd better explain. "Let's take it slowly. For every step in the project there is a time estimate; the length of time, we estimate, it will take from the start of that step until completion of that step. Mark, when you or your people are asked to estimate the time required for a step, how much safety do you embed in your time estimate?"

"No safety. We give realistic estimations. As much as we can." He is not playing games with me, he believes in what he is saying. I don't see any choice but to dive to a deeper level.

"You all learned about probability distributions," I start my explanation.

Knowing the extent to which students dislike statistics I decide to take it in very clear steps all to the point. "Consider a good marksman aiming to hit a bull's-eye and using a well-balanced gun. What is the probability of the marksman hitting a specific point on the target?"

I draw the Gaussian distribution on the board.

"You've probably seen this bell shape more than once." Nevertheless, I explain, "The probability of our good marksman missing the target completely is very low. His probability of hitting the bull's-eye is not one hundred percent, but it's higher than the probability of hitting any other point on the target. And

here is the probability distribution of an excellent marksman."
And I draw a much thinner and taller Gaussian.

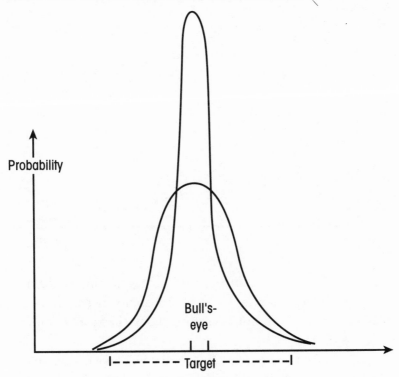

"Now let's consider another case. How much time will it take
you to drive from the university to your house? Brian, would
you volunteer?"

"About twenty-five minutes," he answers, not really knowing what I'm asking for.

"What do you mean by 'about'?"

"About means about. Sometimes it may take thirty minutes,
sometimes less. Depends on the traffic. Late at night, and with
my radar detector on, I might do it in less than ten minutes. In
rush hour on a bad day it might even take an hour." He starts to
see what I mean, because he continues, "If I have a flat tire it
would take more. If my friends persuade me to stop at a bar, it
might take even longer."

Eliyahu M. Goldratt

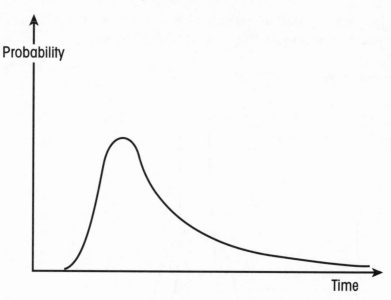

"Precisely," I say, and draw the corresponding probability distribution. Five minutes has zero probability, twenty-five minutes has the highest, but even three hours has some non-zero probability.

"Mark, when you estimate the time it will take to do a step in a project, which one of these two probability distributions more closely resembles your situation?"

"The last one." Grinning, he adds, "Actually it is more like Brian, who loves to stop for a drink and talk for hours."

"The higher the uncertainty the longer the tail of the distribution," I remind them. "This is the median of the distribution," I draw the line on the graph. "It means that there is only a fifty percent chance of finishing at or before this time."

I wait for everyone to digest this fact before I turn back to Mark. "Mark, when Brian was asked to estimate, he gave an estimation that is close to the median. But when you or your people are asked to estimate the time required for a step in a project, what estimation do you usually give? Will you, please, come here and show it to us on Brian's probability distribution."

It takes him some time to reach the board. I hand him the chalk, and without hesitation he draws a vertical line, way to the right of the distribution curve.

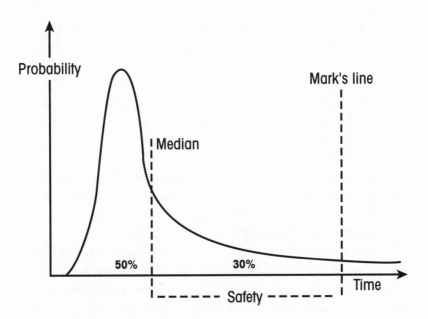

"Why not the median?" I ask him.

"Because Murphy does exist," he laughs.

"It also exists for Brian."

"Come on," he says. "Only a suicidal, inexperienced person would choose the median."

"Makes sense," I comment. "It especially makes sense because in most environments there is little positive incentive, if any, to finish ahead of time, but there are plenty of explanations required when we are late. Under such conditions, I agree with Mark that almost nobody will choose an estimate they have a fifty percent chance of blowing. What probability will you feel comfortable with?"

"Minimum, eighty percent," comes the answer, "preferably ninety."

No arguments.

"Mark, now we understand why you put your time estimate way to the right of the probability distribution. It is somewhere around eighty or ninety percent."

"Sure."

Addressing the class, I declare, "The difference between the median of the probability distribution and the actual estimate is the safety we put in." And I pause to give them time to think it through.

I turn back to Mark. "So, in your time estimates, you do include safety to protect yourself against uncertainty, or in your words, Murphy?"

"I guess so."

"When we compare the time indicated by the median to the time you indicated as a reasonable estimate, it doesn't look like the safety you added is in the range of twenty percent."

"Closer to two hundred percent," he admits.

"Look at the graph," I urge them. "Do you understand that the time estimate that gives us a fifty percent chance is much shorter than the time estimate that provides an eighty percent chance of completing a step before the estimated time? And don't forget, the bigger the uncertainty, the bigger the difference."

"So, two hundred percent safety and more is the norm, not the exception," Ruth says thoughtfully.

"Except for some over-zealous engineers, everybody makes estimates at the range of over eighty percent chance," I say. "Which means that for each and every step of the project we factor in a lot of safety. Are you starting to realize," I ask the class, "the extent to which we do insert safety into our projects?"

They all nod, trying to digest it. Mark returns to his seat, still looking over his shoulder at the probability distribution displayed on the board. I wait until I'm convinced that Mark and the two unfortunate students he tripped over are okay, and start my summary.

"We concluded that the uncertainty existing in every project is the underlying main cause for most problems. Now we see that people are not blind to it and they do add a lot of safety in their planning. Do you agree that we must investigate, more deeply, this issue of safety?"

Full consensus.

"Good," I say. "So here is your homework assignment. Go back to the project you examined and pick, arbitrarily, at least three different steps from that project. For each of the steps you selected find out how the time estimate was arrived at. Don't just ask the project leader. Find out who gave him or her the estimate and interview the source."

Ted raises his hand in apparent discomfort.

"What's the matter, Ted?"

"It's not so simple."

"Why?"

Ted is still looking for words when Charlie answers, "Because, many times a step appearing on the chart of the project leader actually represents many tasks done by many different people."

"Several people are involved in generating the time estimate for even one step in the project," Brian elaborates.

"So you'll have to do some digging," I cynically say.

"Some digging," Ted echoes. "What an understatement. It's a lot of work."

"And most of it is not documented anywhere," Brian continues to express his concerns. "I wonder if people will remember how they derived the original estimates."

"You'll have to do your best," I reply. "Remember, we just concluded that it's vital for us to gain a better understanding of this issue of the safety embedded in the planning of a project. I can tell you that very little exists in the literature about this topic. If we want to make any headway, we'll have to dig up the data ourselves. There is no other choice."

"It's a lot of work," Ted is vocal. "We can't do it for next session."

I try to argue, but there is little you can do against a unified class. It's a problem. I'll have to deviate from the sequence I had planned to follow. On second thought, it won't be too disruptive. I can devote the next session to the subject of PERT and critical path. We compromise, and agree that they will submit the assignment the session after next. At least they promise to do an in-depth job.

Mark, Ruth and Fred are sitting in their tiny office, reading each other's reports. Mark is the first one to finish. He waits patiently for the others. He speaks only after Fred puts his papers on the table. "What do you think?"

"It seems," Ruth slowly says, "that what we have found supports what we've learned in class. People do give their 'realistic estimates' according to their worst, past experience."

"That's what it looks like," Mark agrees. "Except for one over-confident individual. In all other cases, I would say that people tend to give estimates that cover their butts. Maybe Dr. Silver is right, maybe there is a lot of safety. And if so . . ."

"Wait," Fred interrupts him. "That is the impression we got by talking to the engineers."

"And even more so to the purchasing department," Mark must add. "Do you really believe that it takes seven weeks to get a lousy connector?"

"I agree. But I think that you are overlooking something." Fred runs his fingers through his thick black hair.

They wait for him to continue.

"In some of our cases, the work is already completed. And you know what? The original estimates were not far off. Out of the four I checked, in one case the work was reported complete ahead of time. In two it was on time, and in one it was way off. In any case, I didn't see this 'two hundred percent plus' safety."

"Maybe time estimates are a self-fulfilling prophesy?" Ruth speculates.

"What do you mean?" Mark is puzzled.

"Remember what we learned in production?" Ruth asks.

"Ruth," Mark answers desperately, "since we got this lousy

assignment we've learned so many things about so many subjects. Can you be a bit more specific?"

"We saw the same phenomenon in production."

Sighing, Mark begs, "Be much more specific."

"Remember that tall, material manager, the one with the beard?"

"Steve? The creep you had a crush on? Of course I remember. How can we forget?" Fred teases her.

"I didn't have a crush on him. Besides, he is married." She turns back to the subject. "Steve told us that his plant got too many complaints about late deliveries; they had lousy due-date performance. So they started to promise their clients three weeks delivery time instead of two. That gave him the ability to release the work a week earlier."

"And nothing changed," Mark recalls. "They continued to suffer from the same lousy due-date performance."

"They said the work would take two weeks, it took two weeks plus. They added more safety time, and said that it would take three weeks, it took three weeks plus. A self-fulfilling prophecy," Ruth summarizes.

"Yes, but that's because production is different," Fred argues. "In production, most of the time parts spend in the plant they are waiting in queues in front of machines, or waiting for another part in front of assembly. Most of the lead time is not actual production, it's in wait and queue. That's not the case in projects."

"And if Dr. Silver is right, and each step in a project contains so much safety? What then? Then in projects also most of the lead time is wait and queue."

"Ruth. Fred. Calm down. Let's think."

Another half an hour of stormy debate doesn't lead them to any conclusions.

"Can we conclude," Mark tries to put an end to it, "that it looks promising but we don't have enough to turn it into any practical line of action?"

"No," says Fred. "I don't think that our findings confirm that there is a lot of safety."

Before the debate starts again from scratch, Mark suggests a compromise, "Let's gather much more data."

Ruth doesn't agree. "What's the point," she says. "We don't have to assemble more data, it will not help us figure out why we have a self-fulfilling prophesy. We have to think."

"Fine," Mark smiles. "You'll think, we'll assemble more data."

"If in some mysterious way your data proves that there is not so much safety, I'll never forgive you," she warns them.

"Why is it so important to you to be right?" Fred asks. "Just because I teased you about Steve?"

"Forget Steve, I have a much better reason. There must be a lot of safety or we don't stand a chance of reaching the pot of gold. Ten thousand shares. I want them."

"Me, too." Fred smiles. "But I'll bet on our 'around the clock' idea to eventually lead us there."

"Forget it. With the inflated egos of our engineers, it will never work."

"Maybe we'll find a way," Fred says, but even he doesn't seem to have much hope.

"Dr. Silver's safety is much more promising." Ruth stands firm.

Mark doesn't take sides. "Should we report to Isaac Levy that maybe another avenue is starting to open up?" he asks.

"Too early," is Ruth's opinion.

"Much too early." Fred is firm.

Chapter 7

When Chris is shown in, B.J. is behind her desk. He puts her memo in front of her and sits down, not saying a word.

B.J. picks up her memo and pretends to read it, slowly. "Well?" she says at last.

"It's totally unacceptable!" Christopher Page declares.

"Why? Your budget was approved based on a forecast. The forecast proved to be exaggerated by over three hundred students." She is firm. "What's so strange about trimming the budget according to actual registrations?"

"That's not the way to run a business school," he states, making a considerable effort to control his frustration. "We are not a mom and pop grocery store. We cannot and should not change with every small fluctuation. We have to work according to a long-term strategy."

"What long-term strategy?" B.J. softly inquires.

That throws him off balance. There is no strategy, unless one calls the tradition of increasing the budget by fifteen percent each year a strategy. On the other hand, he doesn't want to continue the debate about the future of the business school at this meeting.

"Chris, the business school must trim the budget according to actual registrations," she repeats.

"It's impractical and you know it," he answers impatiently. "The fact that there are fewer students per course does not reduce the cost of giving the class."

"We can reduce the number of courses," she insists.

"Too late," he says, categorically.

"No, it's not," she is as firm. "In the last two years the school has increased the number of elective courses by over fifty percent. You don't have to wait for next year, you can trim some next semester."

"It will be an administrative nightmare," he objects.

Ignoring him, she sails on. "And in so many required courses you are running two or even three parallel classes. Merge them. We can do with fewer adjunct professors."

Twenty minutes later, defeated, Page retreats from B.J.'s office. She is not happy, either. She knows she won just a battle. The business school's committees are still processing recommendations for tenure and are still actively pursuing donations for another building. She has no doubt that if she throws her weight around she can block them.

B.J. makes up her mind. She presses the intercom. "Please get me Bernard Goldsmith," she requests of her secretary.

Bernard picked B.J. up at the airport. When they reached his car, B.J. said, "Let's not go anywhere, just drive."

He is not surprised. They had discussed it before. A car is one of the few places they can have a discussion without being interrupted.

Two minutes later they are on the highway heading away from town. The traffic is light.

"Bernie, I don't know what to do," B.J. almost whispers.

Bernard has known her for a long time. He knows that he doesn't have to help this strong and sharp woman to clarify her dilemma. She wouldn't talk, not even to him, before she verbalized it clearly to herself. She came to him to try and find an answer. So he patiently waits for her to continue. He has to wait for quite some time.

"Remember our last conversation, in Washington?"

"The drop in applicants for our business schools," he says, demonstrating that he remembers.

Of course he does. Being the president of a university, which has a large business school, Bernard is naturally interested in the subject. Not just interested, concerned. He was concerned before the dinner discussion in Washington. The discussion intensified his concerns, but day-to-day responsibilities distracted him. B.J.'s phone call brought it all back.

"I think that at the gathering in Washington we didn't analyze the problem correctly. It's much worse than we suspected," B.J. categorically states.

Regarding B.J. as one of the most forward thinkers in his profession, her last sentence really worries him. Anxiously he waits for her to explain.

"We were concerned about a potential, gradual decline in enrollments at our business schools," B.J. starts her explanation from the very beginning. "In Washington, we said that it was because the business schools' capacity grew, and continued to grow, beyond the market need for MBAs."

"We also said it might be that the word is out that an MBA degree doesn't guarantee a lucrative job anymore," Bernard adds.

"Correct. And since then I've conducted a large survey that verifies it."

"Can I have a copy?"

"Certainly. But Bernard, I'm afraid that we had a conceptual mistake in our explanation. Consciously, or subconsciously, we were extrapolating from the drop that happened in registrations to the law schools. The symptoms are the same, but I'm afraid that the causes are vastly different."

She pauses before she continues. "In law schools they are

going through the normal adjustment between demand and supply. Their problem is that they over-supplied the market needs."

"Over-supply is an understatement. Who needs so many lawyers?"

She ignores his remark. "That is not the case for business. We are not even coming close to supplying the market needs. Over-supply cannot possibly be the cause."

"How do you know?"

"Everybody knows that there is a big shortfall of qualified managers. Couldn't you use some in your organization?"

"If I could get rid of some of my inept buffoons, I definitely could."

She smiles. "Oh, Bernie, it's so good to be with you."

"I will not say 'same here' until you tell me the answer."

"The answer for what?"

"If we aren't over-supplying the market demand, why have we started seeing the same symptoms?"

B.J. becomes tense again. "I didn't say that we aren't over-supplying the market demand, I said that we are not even close to supplying the markets' needs."

"Have mercy on me, stop talking in riddles, I'm just a simple university president," Bernard jokingly begs.

"Bernie, when are we going to open our eyes?" she quietly says.

"Please open them for me," he requests sarcastically.

B.J. doesn't respond. She feels sad. It's so obvious, it's written on all the walls, it hit them in the face, but even Bernie doesn't want to face the obvious. Why impose it on him.

He strokes her hand. "Please." His voice contains only genuine interest. Well, it took her a very long time to face it, too.

In a lifeless tone she starts to explain. "What law students get in law schools is not just a piece of paper but essential knowledge. Do you know of a single person who thinks that one can become a good lawyer without studying?"

"I know people for whom the only good lawyer is a dead

one," he tries to cheer her up. "But I see what you mean. Almost nobody will claim that you can't become a good manager without first having an MBA. You and I don't have MBAs and we manage large organizations."

"In the last few weeks I've used every opportunity to check the opinion of managers about the validity of our teaching. Bernie, it's horrible. There is widespread awareness that it's basically useless."

"Aren't you exaggerating?"

At any other time such a comment would trigger some harsh response from B.J. Any other time Bernard would not think of making such a comment.

"Some managers told me that they are disillusioned to the extent that they are no longer looking for young, bright MBAs. Others told me that they even discourage their people from registering for an MBA program."

Bernard had sufficient time to relate her message to his experience. It matched. Slowly, he says, "What you are claiming is that we are building our grand castles on quicksand."

"Let's face it, Bernie. We don't deliver and the market, to a large extent, already knows it."

They drive in silence for a while. Bernie tries to digest. "But B.J., it can't be. If you are right, nobody would have registered. We charge tens of thousands of dollars, they spend years of their lives, and we don't deliver anything of value? If that were true they would have thrown stones at us. No, B.J., you must be wrong."

"Bernie, what do you want? You want me to say that I'm wrong? You want to convince yourself that I'm just an hysterical woman who is absolutely wrong? But Bernard, what for? It does not change the facts."

At last she reached him. He cannot regard it any longer as a concern, as another item on the agenda. He knows she is right. Almost none of his friends consider an MBA important. He himself, when hiring managers, doesn't consider it as relevant anymore. Still . . .

"B.J., answer me just that. What is saving us from tar and feathers?"

"The respect for higher education," she answers in a lifeless voice. "Respect that is well-deserved by some of our departments but not by others."

It makes sense to him. His mind is racing now, trying to see the ramifications. "When organizations overcome the respect for a university degree the real collapse will happen. I wonder how many business schools will survive then. B.J., we must do something about it. We must save our business schools. They amount to half the university."

"There is nothing to do," B.J. says flatly. "Management is an art and we try to teach it as if it is a science. It cannot work, it doesn't work, and it will never work."

"I don't agree," Bernard is adamant. "It's not art. Organizations have procedures. They operate through defined structures. They institute rules. Management is not based just on impressions and intuition. In organizations many things can even be measured by numbers."

She thinks about it. "You may be right," she says, not willing to argue. "Do you really think that, in its current state, management is like an accurate science?"

"If it were, we wouldn't face the problem," he agrees.

"Do you also agree that we should not count on a miracle? That we should not behave as if we expect business know-how to be turned into science in the near future?"

She doesn't wait for him to agree. "So one thing is clear. We cannot sit around, doing nothing, waiting for the unavoidable collapse of our business schools. Bernard, we must move. It's our responsibility."

"What do you suggest we do?" He speaks so softly she barely hears him.

"There is only one thing that we can and must do. We must start to prudently shrink our business schools."

For another three miles no one says a word. Bernard thinks about what it means. B.J. does the same.

"B.J., I must bitterly thank you, but you didn't fly here just to open my eyes. You have a problem. What is it?"

"Bernie, I'm not up to it," she confesses. "I fought to become the president of a university in order to build. To build a place for young and not-so-young people to grow. Now I know I must slash, that's the only way, still I cannot bring myself to be a butcher."

"I understand," he quietly says. "But B.J., now we both know what will happen if we continue to refuse to address the issue. The business schools will tumble anyway, and if we don't start to trim now, the trauma will be much bigger. The business schools might take down other departments with them. We have responsibility for hundreds, for thousands of people."

"I know. Believe me, I know. But Bernie, I cannot do it. Not even the first step. I tried to bring myself to stop granting tenure. Our business school qualified eight candidates. I read their files. Not much is there, but from the little there is you can see how hard they had to work for it. How many years they devoted. I can picture their families. I can picture how it will ruin them.

"Don't misunderstand me," she adds. "I don't have any problem getting rid of a person who is not carrying his weight. Nobody will accuse me of being softhearted, but these people deserve better. They are good, bright, hard-working people."

"When you are in charge of an omelet you have to break eggs."

"Let somebody else break people," she says bitterly. "I'm thinking of resigning."

B.J. is not a person to say such a thing lightly. With effort, he restrains himself from referring to her shocking statement and says, "You don't break them. You do them a big favor."

She almost chokes.

"Listen to me," he continues in a harsh voice. "Let them get out now. They are young. They are bright. They will carve themselves a good niche. Every year that you allow them to stay diminishes their chances. The market will be less appreciative of their knowledge and they will be less able to adapt."

She doesn't answer. Five minutes later, she puts her hand on his. "Can you please return to the airport. I can still catch the six o'clock flight."

They drive in silence.

When she leaves, she kisses him on the cheek, "Bernie, you are a good friend."

Chapter 8

There's a knock on my door. I raise my eyes from my work and see Jim already coming in with a stack of papers in his hand.

"It's beautiful," he says, and drops them on my desk. "With your twenty-six cases on top of the ones I've gotten in the past two years, we now have plenty for a good article."

He pulls up a chair. "Here are my suggestions for the various sections." He thumbs through the pile and at last hands me a handwritten page. I'm an expert at deciphering Jim's handwriting, but this one is stretching the limit.

"Overdue and overruns," I finally guess the first subtitle.

"Rick, there is a lot of research published on the subject, and for most of our cases we don't have the exact numbers. So, what I suggest is that you assemble the most appropriate references and we'll report that our findings confirm the previous research."

So far it translates into a minimum of two boring days in the library, I note to myself, wondering what is still to come.

"The emphasis should be on categorizing the official and the unofficial reasons for the snafus," he continues. "I've scribbled a list of sections. Feel free to add."

So these serpents are the sections. I hand him back his page, saying, "It's better if we discuss each one of them."

After about twenty minutes I have the full list. I estimate that there are about seventy reports in the pile. How much time will it take me to go over all the reports, doing such an elaborate content analysis? A lot. It's boring work, but I have to do it. I can't give it to one of Jim's Ph.D. students.

But that was the deal. I teach the course and I do the dirty work. Then I have the honor of writing the first draft of the article and the second and the . . . And on each draft Jim's name will appear before mine.

I'd better not think this way. It's actually his course and his idea, and I do need to publish articles. I must stop these negative thoughts and be thankful for the opportunity.

I tell him about the pattern the class discovered: the lower the position of the manager the more the finger points not just outside the company but inside as well.

"Interesting," he comments. He thinks for a little while and then grabs the pile and starts going through it. I turn back to my work. At least ten minutes go by. Jim puts the pile down and starts to pace the room.

"Interesting," he finally says. I refrain from commenting that he had the same opinion fifteen minutes ago.

"Rick, I think that we should make this very interesting finding the center of the article. Our cases certainly back it up. Forty-four different organizations, ranging from non-profit service organizations to industry; seventy-eight different projects, ranging from less than thirty thousand dollars to over three hundred million, and the same pattern appears in almost all of them. Rick, it's great! At last we have something important around which to center this impressive, in-depth survey. We should even choose the title in accordance."

Making so much fuss about such a minute point. But he is the expert on how to dress up an article, so I'm not about to argue. Still . . .

"Jim," I hesitantly start, "there is something else I've noticed, going through the reports." I rifle through the pile trying to find Fred's pages. "Where is it?"

As Jim is about to lose his patience, I find it and hand it over. "Read the financial status."

He locates it quickly. "Okay. 'Due to budget overruns (sixteen point two percent) and delays in production, the original estimate of three years payback is now modified to five.' Typical. What's your point?"

"The budget overrun, being only sixteen point two percent, cannot possibly change the original estimate for the payback period by more than half a year."

"So?"

"But they had to increase the estimated payback period from three years to five. By the way, the person writing it is a project auditor and he claims that his friends are already pushing to change the official estimate to seven years."

Jim still doesn't get it. It's not like him. Patiently, I continue, "If the budget overrun can't possibly cause such a change in the payback period, it must be caused mainly by the delays in completing the project."

"So it seems." He starts to pace again. "So it seems," he repeats. "Let me see. What you claim is that the major, negative financial ramification does not stem from spending too much money."

"Financially, the overruns are much less important than the overdue," I stress.

"In this particular case you are right."

"I found it in six more cases."

"What about all the others?" Jim isn't overly enthused.

"I don't know," I admit. "As you said, for many cases we don't have the numbers for the overruns and overdues, not to mention the payback period."

"Pity," he says, and puts back Fred's report. "It could be an interesting addition, but never mind, we have enough."

"Jim, forget the article for a minute. I think that it is an important point. Important enough to highlight it to the students."

"Peculiar maybe. But important? In what way?"

"In the same report," I don't give up, "it's indicated that they chose the cheap vendors over the more reliable ones. How much do you think they saved?"

"How do I know? Maybe five percent. Can't be much more."

"You can also see," I continue, "that delays in getting the machines from those vendors was the prime reason for the delay in completing the project."

"I see what you mean." He picks up Fred's report again and looks at it intently. Finally, he says, "So they saved about five percent on the machines, which is, probably, less than three percent of the total investment in the project." Very slowly he continues, "And this savings caused them to turn a three-year payback project into . . ." He stops.

"Saving a miserable three percent caused them to turn a very good project into a loser," I summarize.

"Rick, calm down. We have made a lot of assumptions. It's not so simple."

I don't know what he is talking about. The effect is clear. Companies are so immersed in the mentality of saving money that they forget that the whole intention of a project is not to save money but to make money.

Out loud I say, "It's a simple fact that they try to cut the budget by a few percent and cause the payback period to double."

"Yes, I give you that, but it's not so simple. We have to assume a distribution of investment throughout the lifetime of the project. Then we have to assume another distribution of net income from the result of the project, the profit of the Malaysian plant in this case. We should also factor in interest and inflation. Depreciation of the machines and the lifetime of the products that the plant in Malaysia produces. The mathematical modeling will be quite involved." He raises his hand to stop me from replying.

Then he sits down and says, "Tell you what. It's a good idea. Too good to let it pass without checking. Find out what is already published on that subject and if we can find a crack I'll persuade Johnny to do the mathematical work. You know how good he is at that. It might work. Yes, it might."

"Don't you think that we should add it to the survey article? It will enable us to support the mathematical model with some real-life examples."

"We don't have to combine the two things into one article in order to support the model with case studies. As a matter of fact, I can make some telephone calls to my students from last year and you can ask your students. Maybe we can gather enough of the missing data to write a third article."

I'm uncomfortable with it. It shows, because Jim bursts out laughing. "Rick, Rick, when are you going to grow up? Join the real world? You never combine two articles into one; you always try to turn two into more."

He comes around to pat me on the back. "One day we'll make a mensch out of you," and he heads out. As he opens the door to leave he asks, "Did the class rebel because of the homework assignment you gave them?"

"Almost," I smile.

"It will be another excellent article. We are cooking." And with those words of wisdom, he leaves my room.

"Jim, wait a minute. Jim." He doesn't hear. I hurry after him, catch him near the elevators (it's amazing how fast he walks), take him aside, and ask the question that has bothered me since my last brief discussion with Miriam.

"I heard there are some rumors about a budget cut," I'm careful not to reveal my source. "Do you think it might jeopardize my chances of getting tenure?"

"Don't worry, Rick."

"But, I am. You know how important it is to me. I'll never get a third chance."

"Richard, it's okay! You'll get your tenure. You earned it fair and square. Everybody thinks so. I personally checked with everybody on the committee. It's not the tenure that should bother you, it's the promotion to full professor. You are way behind on publications. So will you start to concentrate on what counts? Work on those articles. They are your future."

"And what about the budget cuts?"

"Relax. There are some games between B.J. and the dean. High politics. But, I assure you, it has nothing to do with you." And he disappears into the elevator.

Chapter 9

"How many of you are familiar with PERT and Gantt techniques?"

Almost everybody raises their hand. "What do you mean by 'familiar'?" Ruth asks.

For lack of a better answer I say, "Good working knowledge."

"Then, I'm afraid, I'm not familiar."

"Ruth, I don't mean that you did a Ph.D. dissertation on it. Have you ever come across a Gantt chart?"

"Yes, more than once. Still a brief review would be helpful."

From the look on the other students' faces, I see that Ruth is not the only one who would like a review. Frankly, I didn't expect this; they should have learned the basics in undergraduate courses. I have such a good collection of real charts, with which I could demonstrate every possible configuration. It's a pity I don't have them with me. Should I go to my office to fetch them? It's a waste of valuable time. I'll improvise. No big deal.

"Let's take a very simple example, just enough to demonstrate the concepts."

"Good," Ruth remarks. They all laugh; no student likes complicated examples. Me either.

"Suppose," I start, still not sure of the example I'm going to pick, "the project is to . . . to build a plant. We need to build the building and then to make it functional."

Before Ruth asks me to define "functional," I continue, "To install the electricity lines, the water and compressed air pipes, et cetera. We also need to select and contract the various vendors to build our machines, and allow the vendors enough time to build them. Once the building and the machines are ready, we can install the machines. The plant is now ready."

"Not until you've hired and trained the people," Fred must remind us.

"What's your point?" Ted is less polite than I would have been. "Plenty of other details are not mentioned here, either."

"Let's keep the example simple," I tell Fred, and invite him to come to the board and draw the relevant PERT chart. Confidently he comes to the front. It takes him less than two minutes to draw the diagram.

"Can you invent some time estimates for the various steps?" I ask him.

"With pleasure." Being a financial manager he cannot stop himself from asking, "Do you also want estimates of investments?"

"No need."

I wait until he finishes and returns to his seat. "According to the numbers that Fred picked, it will take ninety days to build the building and thirty days to make it functional. A total of one hundred twenty days."

"Fred, where did you get such unrealistic numbers," Ted shouts.

"Out of thin air," Fred calmly answers.

I ignore them both and continue. "To pick the vendors takes fifteen days."

"Only in Fred's dreams."

I give Ted a look. He signals, "Sorry." I finish my sentence, "And the time it will take them to supply is another ninety days. The installation of machines takes an additional thirty days. What is the critical path?"

"The building." Ted is very vocal today.

"Why?"

"Because, according to Fred's ridiculous numbers, it takes one hundred twenty days to prepare the building while the machines are ready in one hundred five days."

"You are too hasty," I tell him. "Critical path is defined as the longest chain of dependent steps. Longest in time, of course."

"I know," he impatiently says. Then more slowly, "The critical path is the path through the steps of building the building, making it functional and installing the machines in it. A total of one hundred fifty days."

"The critical path," I remind the class, "determines the time it will take to finish the project. Any delay on the critical path will delay the completion of the project. That's why the project manager must focus on it."

Nobody has a problem with what I've said. No wonder, considering their experience in projects.

"If we call the time we start the critical path 'time zero,' the project is planned to be finished at time one hundred and fifty. When should we start the other path? When should we start picking the vendors for the machines?"

"There is no rush there," Brian volunteers an answer. "We can start picking the vendors at time fifteen."

"What?" Ted exclaims.

I signal Ted to calm down and ask Brian to come to the board and draw the corresponding Gantt chart. He does it without any difficulty.

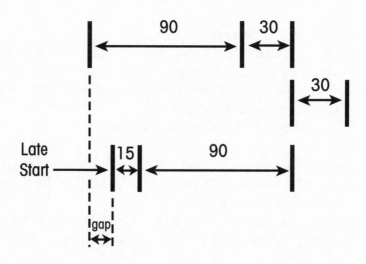

"Brian chose the late start for picking the vendors," I say. "But, as we all heard, Ted probably has another suggestion. But Ted, rather than giving us a whole speech, go to the board and draw your Gantt chart."

That throws him off balance for a second, but just for a second. When his chart is done he turns and starts attacking Brian, "I don't know what's gotten into you. You are going to tell me that in the projects you manage you really start at the latest possible time? No wonder your projects are late. You've got spare time, take it! That's my motto."

"Fine, Ted," I calm him down. "But will you please go back to your seat so we all can see what you drew?

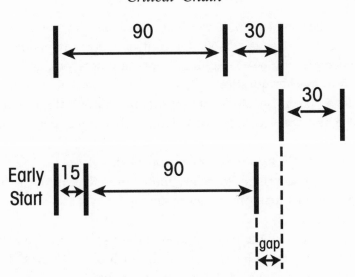

"Gantt charts, unlike PERT diagrams, involve decisions," I highlight to the class, "the decision of the planner when to start each path. Brian chose the late start for picking the vendors while Ted has chosen the early start."

"Of course," Ted almost shouts. "What's the point in taking unnecessary risks!"

"The point is," Fred interjects, "to postpone the investments until they are really necessary. Don't you think that's just as important?"

"I'm not sure," is Ted's response, but it's clear that he is less sure about his position.

"It's an optimization problem," Brian is confident. "We have to weigh the savings from postponing an investment against the chance of damage resulting from finishing the project a little late."

One thing I passionately hate is optimization problems. There are so many articles about these cases, all with involved mathematical models, all so tough and time-consuming to read. And from my experience, all have little practical use. But what can I do; it is an optimization problem.

Ruth raises her hand. Here it comes. Now I'll be forced to

show them the equation and how to solve it. It's going to be a boring and useless lesson. Of course, I don't remember the mathematics by heart. Sighing, I open my notebook and signal Ruth to ask her question.

To my surprise, she starts by saying, "I don't think that it's just a financial consideration. It's much more a management issue."

"Explain." I try not to appear puzzled.

"In a project there are many more paths than in our simplified example; many more entry steps."

"Of course."

"If we start all the paths at their earliest start, don't you think that the project leader will have too much on her hands? From my experience," she adds, "if I start too many things, I'm bound to lose focus, and losing focus is one thing a project leader cannot afford."

I never thought about it this way. To gain time I ask the class, "What do you think?"

"Makes sense," is Charlie's response. "Makes perfect sense. In retrospect, I think Ruth put her finger on the biggest mistake I usually make."

The expressions on most faces indicate they agree with Charlie. Fred maintains his poker face.

"What do you think, Fred?"

"I think that, except for cases where the investment is relatively large, Ruth's argument is much more important than the consideration of postponing an investment."

It takes me some time to realize that he actually agrees with Ruth. Then he explains. "If the project leader loses focus, the project is bound to be very late. The financial penalty of delaying the income from the completed project almost always dwarfs everything else."

Nobody argues. Not even Ted.

"Very nice, Ruth," I congratulate her. "It looks like you hit the nail on the head."

"I haven't finished yet," she declines the compliment. I wait for her to continue.

"Can you repeat what you said about the need to focus on the critical path?" she asks.

I don't have a clue. What is she driving at? But I also don't have any problem repeating myself. "The critical path determines when the project will be finished. Any delay on the critical path will delay the project."

"If we start at the late start, isn't it true for all the other paths as well?" she slowly asks.

I have to think it over. "If we start a path on its late start," I wonder aloud, "then that path doesn't have any time slack. Which means that any delay on that path will also cause a delay in the project."

"Exactly," Ted bursts in. "So if we start everything on its late start, everything becomes important. And I'll have to concentrate on everything. Kiss focusing good-bye."

"Concentrating on everything is synonymous with not concentrating at all," I agree with him. "So where do we stand? If the project leaders use early starts, they will lose focus. If they use late starts, focusing is not possible at all. We have to find the mechanism, the rules, that will enable a project leader to focus."

"Focusing is important," says one of the students, "but there are many other things that are just as important."

"May I say something?" Fred is provoked. He stands up, "In financial auditing we know very well that in projects, once they are approved, there is only one important thing. Not many, just one. If the project manager stays focused, every problem will be solved. If he isn't, we stop expecting benefits, we pray that the losses will not be too big." He makes his point and sits down.

"Anybody else want to comment?"

"Yes," says Mark. I gesture for him to speak up. Two minutes ago I was afraid that this session would turn out to be a boring mathematical drag, now I have an animated discussion on my hands. It's good. That's the way education should be. Connected to real life. Passionate.

Mark clears his throat, and starts, "For those of you who don't intuitively realize how important focusing is, let me remind you that we know that during the project Murphy will strike, and strike more than once. From my experience, I can tell you, if the project leader is not focused or doesn't maintain focus, the emergencies will turn the project into a fiasco."

"Hear, hear." I probably have somebody from England in the class.

"So what are we supposed to do? Early start, no good. Late start, no good."

"Use middle start?" somebody tries to joke.

"Well?" I ask, not knowing the answer.

"I said it all along," Charlie declares, and then clarifies, "I said that we need a much better way to manage our projects."

"That's what we're here for!" Mark's deep voice booms.

What a deep hole I have dug for myself. Maintaining a straight face, I calmly say, "Maybe we can approach it from another angle? A proper control mechanism should keep us focused."

Everybody is quiet because nobody, including me, understands what I actually said. Not for long.

"What do you mean by that?" Ruth asks.

When you are in a hole, stop digging, I remind myself. I'm about to admit that I'm stuck, and highlight that it's not just me but the state of the existing know-how, when I'm saved by the bell. Well, not exactly a bell, but something even louder. Ted.

"It's obvious!" he shouts at Ruth. "Everybody knows what a control mechanism is: it measures the progress of the project. The problem is," he turns to me, "that by the time the progress report indicates something is wrong, it's usually too late."

"Yes," a skinny student, sitting at the end of the second row, supports him.

"What's your name?" I ask.

"Ah . . . Tom."

Before he has a chance to return to his cocoon, I ask him to clarify why he thinks that progress reports usually raise the flag too late.

He doesn't answer. Fred answers for him. "A progress report will tell you that ninety percent of the project is finished in one year and then, the remaining ten percent takes another full year."

The class bursts out laughing.

"It seems like you all share this experience with Fred," I finally manage to say.

Many heads nod.

"In that case," I say, relieved, "we'd better discuss how you monitor the progress of your projects."

It's not long before we get a good handle on how progress is measured in reality. Not much different than what I found in the literature. Progress is measured according to the amount of work, or investment, already done, relative to the amount still to do. In all my students' cases, including the cases where milestones and progress payment were used, this measurement did not differentiate between work done on the critical path and work done on other paths.

"Can anybody predict the impact of measuring progress in this way?" I ask the class.

"We reward starting each path at the earliest possible time," Brian is quick to notice. "This measurement encourages the project leader to start unfocused."

"Moreover," Charlie notices, "it encourages the project leader to continue being unfocused."

"How come?"

"Because according to our measurement," he explains, "progress on one path compensates for a delay on another. So we encourage progressing fast on one path even though another path is delayed."

"What's bad about that?" Mark asks. "If I have difficulties in one path, why shouldn't I move on the other paths where I can?"

"At the end they all merge together," Charlie reminds him.

"All the advance that you gain in the open paths will have to wait for the delayed path anyway. You made the investment too early, and what is worse, you allowed yourself to not concentrate on the place you should, on the delayed path that needs your attention."

Mark doesn't answer. It looks like he's doing some soul-searching.

"A shortsighted project manager," Charlie's still talking to him, "can ignore the paths that are slowed down by problems, and the measurement will still indicate that the project is progressing. The project leader looks good. For a while. A long while. Only when the work is complete on all the other open paths, and only the problematic path remains, only then will the fallacy start to be revealed. Mark, don't see this as personal criticism. I do exactly the same thing. Only in the last fifteen minutes have I become so smart."

"Thank you," says Mark. "But I still have to think about it."

I don't hurry to break the silence. It's not every day this happens to a professor. Students learning something very important that they can use. Learning and acknowledging it. Actually, it's the first time for me.

No wonder I'm slightly irritated when Fred bursts out with "Now, I finally understand."

"What?" I'm a little too snappy.

"Now I understand why so many projects take so long to complete their last ten percent. It's because, in measuring progress, we overlooked the importance of the critical path. I found the enemy, it is me. I'm the one who prepares all the project progress reports!"

What a class!

I turn into my driveway and hit the brakes as fast and hard as I can. Slightly shaken, I step out of my car and check the front. I doubt if there is enough space to slip a cigarette paper between my car and the shiny Chevy Blazer. It has temporary plates. Why didn't Judith warn me we were having guests for dinner?

I walk around this magnificent piece of engineering. It's my dream. A sports-utility vehicle, four-wheel drive. A big, roomy, strong car. An unattainable dream, at least for now. This baby cost almost as much as my yearly income. I go into the house.

No guests. Judith is taking a shower. The table is set for two. There are big red candles on the table. Candles! I hurry back to the Blazer and check the registration in the glove compartment. What am I going to do now? It's gone too far! I go back into the living room and fix drinks for two. Then I sit on the couch and wait.

Finally, she comes down. She is beautiful. New hairdo. I'm not sure about the earrings, but I do recognize the dress. She sits near me, takes her drink, and looking at the golden liquid asks, "How do you like your present?"

So, it's my present.

"Do you like the color? Silver is our color, don't you think?"

I take another sip.

"I know how much you want a sports-utility. It's about time you had a decent car."

"I could wait."

"Your car is falling apart," she sits herself in my lap.

It won't work. Not this time. "Judith, how are we going to pay for it?"

"Honey, we'll manage." She brushes my cheek with her lips.

I try to bring her back to reality. "We can't afford it," I say.

"Oh baby, we can." She loosens my tie, and works on my shirt buttons . . . "You're getting tenure and, as you've told me so many times, it won't be long before you become a chaired professor." She strokes my chest.

I grab her shoulders, push her slightly away, and repeat slowly, emphasizing each word, "Right now we cannot afford to buy it!"

She looks at me, then she stands up. "Rick, since the day we got married, I've been hearing the same thing. We cannot afford it. We cannot afford it. I can't listen to it any longer! I waited years for you to finish your studies. I didn't make a face when your friends made a bundle while you continued in academia. But enough is enough. I want to live. Now."

"Judith, be realistic. The fact is that right now we cannot afford it. You know how much we borrowed. You know we can't afford a secondhand Subaru and you go out and buy a brand new Chevy Blazer?"

"Listen, Richard Silver," she put her hands on her hips. "I don't want to hear it anymore. I don't want you to tell me that we cannot afford it now, that we have to wait, that someday . . ."

"But, Judith," I try to calm her down, "that's life."

"Life! You dare to talk to me about life! I'm not going to listen to you anymore." She starts to cry. "I've listened once too often."

It hurts. Years ago I said "We cannot afford a child. Not now." A year ago Judith found out that she can no longer have children. I stand up and hug her. Hugs are lousy compensation. So is a new house. Or a Chevy Blazer.

Chapter 10

"Not bad for a first draft." Jim drops our article on my table. "I marked some of the points that need a little work."

The first page looks like it is suffering from a severe case of the measles. I glance at the rest. The disease has spread throughout all the pages. Even the tables are contaminated. I'm not surprised. That's what I expect from meticulous Jim. Sighing, I put it back on the table.

"It's going to be a nice piece of work," he encourages me. "I don't see much of a problem getting it past any editor."

"Can we expect to see it published before the end of this academic year?"

"If we are lucky. But that's not the point. This article is going to be published, for sure. What you need is many more. By the way, I've talked with Johnny about modeling the financial impact of project overdues."

"And?"

"And he is not interested."

I'm quite surprised. It's not like Johnny. Since when is he declining the opportunity to develop a mathematical model?

But knowing Jim's power of persuasion, there is no point trying to talk to Johnny myself. "So what are the options?" I ask, a little bit discouraged.

"You can wait until I find the time and stamina to do it. . . ." Considering the fact that it isn't Jim's idea, it means waiting forever. "Or you can do the mathematical work yourself." No way. "It's as simple as that."

"There is a third alternative," I say. "I can come up with some new ideas."

"And give up on highlighting the financial impact of overdues? I don't understand you, Richard. You make so much fuss about the futility of most articles. If it weren't for the fact that I practically forced you to write some things with me, you wouldn't be published at all. At last you came up with something that even you consider practical, something that we can turn into not one, but two articles, and now you want to give it up? Just because you have to figure out the math?"

He examines my poker face, and almost disgusted, he adds, "Besides, where are you going to find good, new ideas."

"I have. Two."

He is on a roll. "Four years of complete drought and now, all of a sudden, I have to assume that you got a flood of inspiration? Will you please wake up."

"I have ideas for two important articles," I repeat.

"You have ideas for two articles?" He mockingly uses his little finger to clean his ear. "Say it again."

I keep a straight face.

"Let's hear them." Jim is skeptical, almost angry.

"With pleasure. But first, let me tell you where these inspirations are suddenly coming from. They are not my ideas; they are ideas that pop up in the brainstorming I'm doing with my class."

"Ahhh," his expression reveals that it makes sense to him. "Those type of ideas."

"What do you mean?" I'm somewhat offended. Never mind, he signals with his hand.

"The first idea," I start to explain, "revolves around the problem of early start versus late start."

"You? You want to deal with an optimization problem? And that's what you call an important article?" He stands up, and pacing, he tries to knock some sense into my skull. "Do you know how many articles have been written about it? The best mathematical brains in the field have been toying with the minute details for years, how can you expect . . ."

I'm counting. Five questions in a row. Jim is pretty impatient today. Finally, he notices my expression and stops. "You have an idea on how to approach it from a totally different angle!" he speculates.

When I confirm it, he starts to listen. I talk; he asks some relevant questions; I answer. He asks some more.

"Let me see if I understand you, Rick. Dozens, maybe hundreds of articles deal with the question of early start of a non-critical path versus late start. Regarding all these articles, in which tremendous efforts and brain power have been invested, you claim something very simple. You claim that it's all a waste of time!"

He pauses to allow me to speak. I open my mouth to answer, but what can I say? To say, "yes" is too arrogant, but I'm not willing to give any other answer.

"You claim it," Jim speaks for me, "because you think that they have concentrated on minor considerations and neglected the major ones."

Before I have a chance to agree, he continues. "You claim that the main thing is the ability of the project manager to focus. You further claim that both early start and late start jeopardize the ability to focus, even though to different degrees. And then, you conclude that ignoring it is ignoring the heart of the problem."

I open my mouth to explain why, but he doesn't wait. "As strange as it may sound, I agree with you. One hundred percent."

I close my mouth.

"I went to all this length to show you that I do understand. Now let me tell you, I'm disappointed."

I'm tired of imitating a fish, so I keep quiet.

"Don't you see that this, how shall I call it, intriguing observation, is totally impractical?"

This is too much. Then I realize he is right. "As long as we are unable to recommend when to start each path, it does have limited practical use," I admit.

"You don't get it, do you?" Jim shakes his head.

Apparently I don't.

"Look Rick," he starts patiently, "you cannot describe focusing of a person by an equation."

"So?"

"So, this problem can't be solved mathematically."

I still don't get it. "But it can be solved logically," I insist. "We now know where to look. If we keep on thinking we might find a logical procedure. It will be immensely helpful for projects."

He is not convinced. I try harder. "Jim, I don't want to sound presumptuous, but I always dreamt of finding such a breakthrough. Something as powerful as Just-In-Time or TQM. They are not based on math, either. These methods are so robust because they are based on common sense, on logical procedures. I know we are still far from reaching the breakthrough, we don't have the answer. But at last we have identified the right problem. You must admit, it's a major step forward."

"It won't help," he sighs.

"You've lost me," I say sincerely.

"Rick, you entered the academic world over ten years ago. It's about time you knew the rules. If you want to move ahead you must publish, and to publish you have to conform to the accepted academic standards. You know the criteria for articles. They must be based on surveys or on mathematical models. That's it."

"But, Jim, what about things like JIT and TQM? According to what you say, they are not academic enough. Still, we teach them in every university."

"They've passed the test of reality."

"But what about new such breakthroughs?"

"If you find one, you can always publish it in a book. Books don't pass through the screening of academic reviewers. But remember, books don't count toward full professorship."

"I know all that. But it's ridiculous!"

"Why?"

"Jim, you yourself have said to me more than once that the knowledge in almost every aspect of organizations is far from being satisfactory. At the same time there is a whole army of people who are supposed to improve it. How many professors are there in business schools around the world? A hundred thousand? And what have we produced? Nothing. In the last thirty years knowledge has progressed in leaps and bounds. How many of those breakthroughs came from academia? Zilch. Don't you see that the criteria we use to judge what is acceptable research are the problem. They choke us. It's almost impossible to put any meaningful contribution through the system. How can we . . ."

He raises his hand to stop me from continuing. "You may not like it, I don't like it, but in order to prevent academic anarchy we all must adhere to the standards. It's like democracy or our legal system. They may suffer from major flaws but they are the best we have."

He glances at his watch. "What about your other idea?"

"Forget it," I say bitterly. "It's important for projects, very important. But it's impractical. It's not based on mathematical models."

"Still, I would like to hear it," he requests gently.

"What for?" Nevertheless, knowing that Jim has a particular interest in measurements, he published a book on them, I say, "It's about how we measure the progress of projects. The measurement is wrong."

"How did you conclude that?" He is genuinely interested. "Did you use my criteria?"

"Yes, of course." And I quote from memory, " 'Criteria number one: Measurements should induce the parts to do what is good for the system as a whole.' Well, the way we measure the progress of a project, the measurement does almost the opposite.

" 'Criteria number two: Measurements should direct managers to the point that needs their attention.' In projects the measurement steers the project leader away. It's ridiculous, it's damaging, and in my opinion, it often leads to the failure of major projects. But it's not important enough to be accepted as a respectable academic article."

He smiles at me and says softly, "You have to cool down. I suggest you go and speak with Johnny Fisher. He can help you."

"Yeah, sure." The last thing I need is another lecture on the importance of optimization techniques.

"It's not what you think," he responds to my expression. "Johnny was on sabbatical last year, but not at another university. He spent the year at UniCo."

"And using his mathematical skills he pretended to save that conglomerate a fortune. Good for him."

"Will you please stop announcing your views on business professors," Jim laughs. "Johnny learned a new method there. Something that, I'm sure, you'll find fascinating. It's all about constructing logical procedures. Exactly what you are looking for. Analysis based on cause-effect relationships, resolutions based on conflicts between necessary conditions, structured common sense, no mathematics."

What is he talking about? I don't really care.

"You don't care, huh? No problem. Just make sure you're at the next faculty colloquium. Johnny is giving it."

Big deal.

Chapter 11

Rick is among the last to enter. To his surprise, the small auditorium is almost full. Probably the word went around that this colloquium was going to be different. Much different. Jim is waving at him. "I kept a seat for you." Now he won't be able to sneak out after fifteen minutes.

"Thanks."

He has just sat down when Johnny Fisher starts.

"I was sitting here watching this auditorium fill up, and I was thinking to myself, all these people came to see me. How flattering. I'm a celebrity. Then I realized, the Ph.D. students are here because they have to be. The professors are here out of courtesy. And all our important guests from industry came, not because of me, but because of the title of my presentation. Well, that's life."

Rick joins the polite laughter.

Johnny leaves the podium and starts to pace the stage. "I was asked to talk about the new things I learned during my one-year sabbatical at UniCo. I must warn you, one year doesn't make one an expert. It is barely enough time to formulate some impression. And that's all I will be able to share with you, impressions."

"Excellent," Rick thinks to himself, "even Johnny wouldn't refer to mathematical models as 'impressions.' On second thought, with Johnny Fisher, nobody knows. Better wait and see."

"UniCo is very famous today. This conglomerate, as you well know, is exhibiting unheard of growth and profits. It is of particular interest to our community since they are building a major high-tech operation here. Their growth is not just in their high-tech subsidiaries, but in all their businesses. Every single one of them. My grant had a hefty travel budget, so believe me I checked."

"That's what I call a grant." Rick is probably not the only professor who had this thought cross his mind.

"It's apparent that they have embarked on a different way to manage their business," Johnny continues with his introduction. "And they don't hide it. They call it Theory of Constraints, or for those of us who love three-letter acronyms, TOC. But what is TOC? That's what I've tried to get a good grasp of. Not the details, but the concept, the framework."

Rick, like everybody else, has heard more and more about TOC in the last ten years or so. What he has heard and read made a lot of sense, but it kept changing. At first it was related to production scheduling. Then it became a banner to attack "product cost" methods. Then marketing. Lately, it seems TOC is more connected with methods to remove friction between people. If Johnny could provide some order for this mess, it might be worthwhile sitting for a hour. Not much more than an hour.

"My impression is," Johnny says, as he turns on one of the overhead projectors, "that TOC is a blend of three different, yet related, breakthroughs."

He puts up his first transparency. "The first one, as we all suspected, is that TOC is actually a new management philosophy."

"Another one of those," Rick whispers to himself.

"In the past ten years," Johnny echoes Rick's discomfort as he resumes his pacing, "we came to know many new management philosophies. They came one after the other: TQM, JIT, re-engineering, the learning organization. . . . At first it looked like we were moving from one fad to another. It was confusing. Nobody liked it. Especially not us, the professors, who all of a sudden were forced to update our course material at an unprecedented pace.

"But then we started to realize that each one had its important contribution. Moreover, not like fashions of the past, all these philosophies are not contradicting each other. On the contrary, in many ways they are complimentary. Many started to believe that they all are just pieces of the same puzzle. Now that I have been intimately exposed to TOC, I think I know. They actually are. And in a much more fascinating way than we suspected. I'm going to demonstrate it."

He moves back to the overhead projector and points to the second line. "The second, and most important breakthrough of TOC, at least in my eyes, is the research methods it introduces. Methods that were adapted from the accurate sciences, adapted to fit systems that contain, not just atoms and electrons, but human beings.

"And the third breakthrough is, of course, the one TOC is known for the most, its broad spectrum of robust applications."

He pauses, goes back to the podium and points to the three sentences on the screen. "New management philosophy, new research methods and robust applications. I think the best way to demonstrate them all is by raising the question, 'What is the biggest problem managers are facing today?' Anybody care to answer?"

A white-haired person in the front row is the first to answer, "How to win against the competition!"

Rick doesn't recognize him. He must be some hotshot from industry. But his answer, as trivial as it might sound, makes sense.

"Any other answers?"

"My opinion is different," says another top manager. "I think that the real problem is how, exactly, we should go about inducing our people to improve. We hear so much about the importance of empowerment, communication, teamwork. At the same time we hear so little about how to actually achieve it."

"He has a point," Jim whispers in Rick's ear. Rick is not so sure.

"In my company, we know exactly how to handle the competitors, and we don't have any problem inducing our people to improve. Our problem is how to shrink the development time of new products. Does TOC have an answer to this problem? If so, I'm very interested."

"So am I," Rick thinks, and whispers to Jim, "Who is that guy?"

"That's Pullman, the chairman of Genemodem," Jim tells him. "Some of their people are in our program."

"My problem is different," says the person sitting next to Pullman. "My biggest problem is my clients. They drive us crazy."

More answers are coming from all directions. Johnny raises his hands. "Please, that's enough. I'm sure that all your answers have merit, but let's not forget the subject of this presentation."

When it becomes quiet, he continues. "TOC regards what was said here as just symptoms. It claims that they all stem from one, single core problem. If true, this is a very profound statement. How am I going to prove it?"

He starts to pace again. "Let me start with the observation that most managers want to manage well; I don't know many who come to work each morning saying 'How can I mess things up today.' But what does it mean, to manage well? Many things. For our discussion, we don't have to list them all. It's enough to agree that two things are absolutely necessary conditions. In order to manage well, managers must control cost, and at the same time, managers must protect throughput—they must ensure that the right products will reach the right clients in a way that they will pay for them."

He stops, faces the audience, and using his hands extensively, he elaborates. "Suppose that one of your managers tells you that he has done an excellent job of controlling cost, that he cut expenses by twenty percent. By the way, he also enraged half your clients. Would you call him a good manager? Or, another one protected throughput, shipped everything on time, but for that he hired more people and put everybody on endless overtime. Good manager?"

"I didn't know Johnny was such a good speaker," Rick comments to Jim, who gives him a look that says, I told you so.

"Controlling cost and protecting throughput. Two absolutely necessary conditions. We cannot be satisfied with one without the other.

"What I would like to show you now is that each implies a different mode of management. So different that there is no acceptable compromise between the two. To demonstrate it let me use an analogy. Let's view your company as a chain. A physical chain. It's not difficult to see why such an analogy makes sense."

He goes to the overhead and puts up a blank transparency. "One link, the purchasing department, is in charge of bringing the materials. Another department, another link, is in charge of starting production. Another department, another link, is in charge of finishing production." As he speaks he draws ovals representing the links. A chain starts to form on the screen.

"Yet other links are in charge of shipping, getting the clients, invoicing and collecting." The chain becomes longer.

He puts the marker down and asks, "What is analogous to 'cost' in our physical chain?" Without waiting, he asks another question. "What typifies cost? Cost is drained by each and every department. We pay money to and through our purchasing department, our production departments, and so forth. No department is free. And if we want to know the total cost of the organization, one way to find it is to sum up the cost drained by each department."

He pauses to check if the audience is with him. Satisfied, he continues, "In our chain, the closest thing to cost will be weight, each link has its weight. And if we want to know what the total weight of the organization is, one way to find out is to sum up the weight of all the links. What are we going to do with this analogy?"

"That's what I want to know," Rick whispers impatiently.

"We are going to use it," Johnny answers, "to demonstrate that controlling cost implies a certain way of managing." And without delay he continues. "Suppose that you are the president in charge of the entire chain. I'm working for you. I'm in charge of a specific department, a specific link. Now you instruct me to 'improve!' And I am obedient. After some time I come back to you and tell you that with ingenuity, of course with ingenuity, and also time and money, I improved my link. I made it one hundred grams lighter. You are not interested in my link, you are interested in the whole chain. But when I tell you that I reduced the weight of my link by one hundred grams you know that the entire chain becomes lighter by that amount. Do you know what that implies?"

Rick doesn't.

"It implies a management philosophy. It implies that any local improvement automatically translates into an improvement of the organization. Which means that to achieve the global improvement, the improvement of the organization, we know that we have to induce many local improvements. I call it the 'cost world.' " He pauses.

"What is he talking about?" Rick is irritated. "Why so much fuss about something first-year students know?"

"Wait," Jim whispers back. "Johnny must have some point here, even though I don't see it yet."

"You're probably wondering," Johnny is smiling, "why I am hammering on the obvious. But it is so trivial to all of us not because it's the only management philosophy, but because it's the management philosophy we all used for so long. We have managed according to the 'cost world' probably since the beginning of the industrial revolution."

He raises his voice. "What is not common knowledge is that 'protecting throughput' implies a contradictory philosophy. It implies the 'throughput world.' What is that?"

Everybody is now quiet. Even Rick.

"First, let's clarify to ourselves the essence of throughput." Pointing to the chain on the screen, Johnny explains: "One link is purchasing, another starts production, another finishes production, another assembles, still another ships to clients, et cetera. If one link, just one link, drops the ball, what happens to the throughput of the company?"

"Drops," many answer.

"When we deal with throughput, it is not just the links that are important; the linkages are just as important."

Rick finds himself nodding in agreement.

"What is the equivalent of throughput in our physical chain? What is determined not just by the links, but by the fact that they interact with each other? It's not weight. If we remove all interaction, all linkages, and we are left with just a pile of links, the weight is still the same. So what property typifies a chain? It is the strength of the chain. If one link breaks, just one link, the chain is broken; the strength of the chain drops to zero.

"Now, I have some seemingly trivial, but very important questions for you. What determines the strength of a chain?"

"The weakest link," somebody in the front answers loudly.

"And how many weakest links do we have in a chain?" Johnny stresses the word 'weakest.'"

"One."

Rick doesn't like Johnny's style. He would never stress such trivialities. But he must admit that it's effective. Johnny now has everybody's attention.

"Now," Johnny says, in an invigorating voice, "now, let's see what that implies. You are still the president in charge of the entire chain. I'm still in charge of just one department. Since there is only one weakest link, let's take the more general case, the case where I'm in charge of a department that is not the weakest link. And . . . and once again you tell me to improve. To improve the strength this time. And once again I come back and report to you that with ingenuity and time and money I improved. I strengthened my link. I made it three times stronger. Give me a medal."

He pauses and smiles. "Remember, you are not really interested in my link. You are interested in the chain. My link wasn't the weakest. If I made my link stronger, how much did I improve the strength of your chain? Nothing. Absolutely nothing."

Jim looks at Rick. "I told you." Rick doesn't respond. His mind is racing.

"Don't you see what we are facing now?" Johnny starts to pace again. His strides are full of energy. "Most of the local improvements do not contribute to the global!" he almost shouts. "And we do want the global, we do want the organization as a whole to improve. Now we know that since any improvement requires attention and time and money, the way to improve the total organization is definitely not through inducing many local improvements, the more the better. That's not the way."

"Interesting," Jim says to himself.

"So where do we stand? In order to control cost, managers must manage according to the 'cost world,' while in order to protect throughput they must manage according to the 'throughput world.' Can they manage according to both at the same time?"

Nobody volunteers even a speculation.

"We try," Johnny sighs. "We definitely try. For example, are you familiar with the term, 'the end of the month syndrome'?"

Many laugh. Especially the guests from industry.

"At the beginning of the month," Johnny explains, "we control cost. Tight fist on overtime. Batch sizes must be optimal. But at the end of the month, forget it. Do everything to ship the damn goods out the door. Expedite these three pieces, go on overtime for the entire weekend. Ship!"

Johnny lowers his voice. "What happens? At the beginning of the month these companies are managed according to the cost world, at the end of the month according to the throughput world.

"Fewer and fewer of these companies survive today. Why? Because compromises that were acceptable yesterday are intolerable today. And not because we have become more fussy, but because our clients have. Ten years ago we shipped eighty percent on time and everything was okay. Today we ship ninety-five percent on time and they still dare to bitch and moan. Ten years ago we shipped the best quality we could produce. Today if we ship that same quality our clients will ship it back. Protecting throughput has become much harder. The margins that enabled us to live with compromises are no longer there.

"But let me prove to you that there is no compromise between the cost world and the throughput world. Not even theoretically. Do you want to see the proof?"

"Yes," the auditorium echoes.

Johnny takes a handkerchief out of his pocket and wipes his forehead.

"For that, I first have to direct your attention to another topic. That of focusing."

Rick straightens in his chair. Maybe he can pick up a clue that will help in his subject.

"We all know that focusing is important." Johnny speaks softly. "A manager who does not know how to focus will not succeed in controlling cost and will not protect throughput. But what is focusing for us? We have come to know it as the Pareto principle. Focus on solving twenty percent of the important problems, and you'll reap eighty percent of the benefits. This is a statistical rule. But those who teach statistics know that the twenty-eighty rule applies only to systems composed of independent variables; it applies only to the cost world where each link is managed individually.

"What about the throughput world? Since in our organizations we do have many more than five links, it's obvious that improving twenty percent means that many of these improvements will not contribute to improving the performance of the organization as a whole. Linkages are important, the variables are dependent. The Pareto principle is not applicable.

"So how can we find out on what to focus? What process can we use?"

"Interesting," Jim says again. This time Rick is in total agreement.

"Well, it's simpler than expected," Johnny comforts them. "Just think about the chain and the fact that its strength is determined by its weakest link. If you want to strengthen the chain, what must your first step be? No 'ifs,' no 'buts,' no 'we are different.' What must be the first step?"

At this stage everybody has probably figured it out. Johnny gestures to a volunteer in the first row to say it out loud, "First thing is to find the weakest link."

"Correct," says Johnny. And grasping a marker, he comments, "In academia we must use more respectable words. So let me write the first step as: IDENTIFY the system's constraint(s). Don't you agree that 'identify' sounds much more impressive than a simple 'find'? Of course these two words mean exactly the same thing. Fine, we identified the constraint. Now what?"

"Strengthen it," the same, first-row person says.

"Correct again," Johnny smiles at him. "But wait. We have to be careful with analogies. When we move back to organizations we can easily see that there are two different cases. The first one is the case where we identify the constraint as physical, like a bottleneck, a type of resource that does not have enough capacity to meet the demand. In that case, strengthening the weakest link will mean to help the bottleneck to do more.

"But we shouldn't overlook the other case. The case where it turned out that the constraint we identified is an erroneous policy. In that case, strengthening the weakest link cannot be interpreted as helping the erroneous policy to do more. We have to replace the policy. By the way, this fork of physical constraints and policy constraints caused a lot of confusion about TOC. All the early publications concentrated on physical constraints. It's no wonder that when articles and books first appeared about the applications to policy constraints, it took some time until we, at least in academia, understood the connection."

"I didn't, until now," Rick admits.

"Interesting," is the only word Jim is willing to say.

Johnny waits for the murmur to quiet down. "At this point I'll stick to physical constraints. They are less important but easier to understand. 'Strengthen the weakest link,' we said. Before I write the second step, I would like to highlight that there are two different ways to strengthen a bottleneck. One is to simply add more capacity, by hiring more people or buying more machines. But there is another way. To squeeze the maximum from the capacity we already have. Make sense?"

When he gets agreement, he continues, "Since TOC accepts 'controlling cost' as an absolute necessary condition, no wonder that it elects the second step to be: Decide how to EXPLOIT the system's constraint(s).

"What next? Let's not forget that in the throughput world the linkages are as important as the links. Which means that if we decided to do something in one link, we have to examine the ramifications on the other links. Once again, it's quite easy. Our intuition is in the throughput world. Always was. Let me demonstrate it to you."

He points to his "volunteer" and tells him, "You'll be the bottleneck. Do you mind? It means that you are most important, the throughput of the entire company depends on you. It also means that you are in the hot seat."

"I'm used to the hot seat."

"Fine. Now let's suppose that when you try, really try, you can produce ten units an hour. No more. Okay?"

Johnny picks another victim. He picks Pullman. "And suppose that you are a non-bottleneck. You can easily do twenty units an hour. But whatever you do, before we can sell it, it must be further processed by our bottleneck. On an ongoing basis, how many units per hour should you produce?"

"Ten units," Pullman says without hesitation.

Johnny repeats the description of the scenario and asks again, "Everybody tell me. How many units an hour should this gentleman produce? Everybody!"

"Ten," comes the roaring answer.

"What you said is the third step." And while talking, he writes it down. "Step three: SUBORDINATE everything else to the above decision. If we can squeeze only ten units from the bottleneck there is no point in doing more on the non-bottlenecks. Now, if this first gentleman is still a bottleneck and we do want more throughput, we must lift some of the load from his shoulders. Even if it means buying more machines or hiring more people."

When everybody agrees, he writes the fourth step: ELEVATE the systems' constraint(s).

Rick carefully copies the steps. The logic is impeccable. It must be applicable for project management as well. Exactly how? It's not clear. He will have to think about it later.

Johnny puts down the marker and moves to the front of the stage. "This is not the last step. And you all, intuitively, know it. Here is our chain." In the air Johnny stretches an imaginary chain between his hands. "Here is the weakest link. I strengthen this link. The whole chain becomes stronger. I strengthen it again, the chain becomes even stronger. I strengthen it again, Nothing happens. Why?"

Many people answer.

Johnny summarizes, "It's not the constraint anymore. So, I have to avoid inertia and go back to step one. Have you noticed something fascinating?"

He pauses, but nobody volunteers to read his mind.

"We have found the process to focus. This is the focusing process of the throughput world. But at the same time, do you agree with me that these steps are also the 'process of on-going improvement'?" Fascinating, isn't it? In the throughput world, focusing and process of on-going improvement are not two different things, they are one and the same."

"Interesting," Rick whispers to Jim.

"No, Rick, Johnny is right. It's fascinating."

"Let me remind you," Johnny returns to the podium, "that I still owe you something. I owe you the proof that there is no acceptable compromise between the cost world and the throughput world. Remember? Now it's easy. Really easy."

He turns back to his volunteers. "You are still the bottleneck. You can produce maximum ten units an hour. And you are still the non-bottleneck, you can easily do twenty an hour, but whatever you do must pass through him. Everybody, again, how much should he produce per hour?"

By now everybody likes his dynamic style. "Ten," they all roar.

"Really?" He cocks his head slightly, still looking at them. "Do you really mean it?"

"Yes." Everybody is confident.

"And I thought that you liked this gentleman." He turns directly to Pullman. "Imagine that you are a worker in your own company. And you produce only ten units per hour when you can easily produce twenty. What will be your recorded efficiencies?"

Understanding starts to spread on Pullman's face. "Low," he says. Then, clearing his throat, "My efficiency will be fifty percent."

"And if your efficiencies are only fifty percent, what will happen to your head?" And smiling, he moves his hand across his neck.

When the laughter quiets somewhat, Johnny continues, "And

everybody here told you to produce only ten. Your friends probably want to turn you into a kamikaze. Some friends."

Johnny is smiling. The laughter reaches new heights.

He waits patiently. "Do you understand what we have seen here? Your intuition is in the throughput world and in this world the answer is 'don't dare to produce more than ten.' But your systems are in the cost world. Your systems want him to reach maximum local efficiency; they want him to produce twenty." He pauses.

"And there is no compromise. If this gentleman produces fifteen, both worlds will kill him."

The message is serious, but everybody laughs.

"So what will he do? He will slow down. He will claim that he cannot produce more than, let's say, twelve, which he will. We forced him to lie, because if he doesn't, his job security is threatened."

Slowly Johnny goes back to the podium. He stands there awhile before resuming his lecture. "Everybody knows that the first step in solving a problem is to define it precisely. The strange thing is that in spite of this realization, we didn't bother defining what we mean by 'defining a problem precisely.' "

He notices that not everybody understands, so he clarifies. "When do we know that we have defined a problem precisely? When we have already solved it, and looking back we agree that the stage when we defined the problem precisely was a major step forward. But how do we know that we defined the problem precisely before we solved it?"

"He has a point," Rick says to Jim.

"TOC adopts the definition accepted in the accurate sciences. A problem is not precisely defined until it can be presented as a conflict between two necessary conditions."

He pauses to let his peers digest.

"That's what we have done for the last half an hour." He goes back to the overhead projector and inserts a transparency.

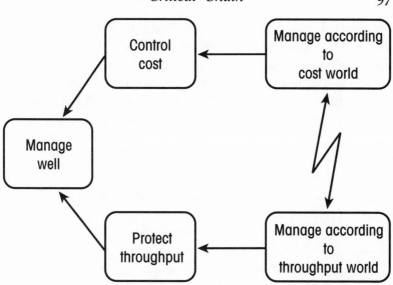

"The objective of managers is to manage well. In order to manage well, one of the necessary conditions is to control cost and the other is to protect throughput. But in order to control cost, managers must manage according to the cost world, while in order to protect throughput they must manage according to the throughput world, and as we saw, these two are in conflict.

"What do we do? We try to find a compromise. And if there isn't one? Life is a bitch.

"Is there any other way? Do they do anything differently in the accurate sciences?"

Everybody waits for Johnny to supply the answer.

"For example," Johnny tries to clarify his point, "suppose that they try to measure the height of a building. Using one method they find that the height is ten yards, and using another the answer comes out to be twenty yards. A conflict. Do you think that they will try to compromise? That they will say that the height of that building is fifteen yards?"

Everybody is grinning.

"In the accurate sciences, what do they do when they face a conflict? Their reaction is very different than ours. We try to find an acceptable compromise. This thought never crosses their minds. Their starting point will never allow it; they don't accept that conflicts exist in reality.

"No matter how well the two methods are accepted, a scientist's instinctive conclusion will be that there is a faulty assumption underlying one of the methods used to measure the height of the building. All their energy will be focused on finding that faulty assumption and correcting it.

"Should we do the same?"

He pauses, and then asks, "Can we do the same?"

As he returns to the podium he keeps on asking, "Can we, who deal with human-based systems, believe that conflicts cannot exist?

"How can we? Conflicts are all around us."

In a conversational tone he continues, "This is probably the most daring assumption of TOC. One of its foundations is that whenever we witness a conflict, it is a clear indication that someone has made a faulty assumption, a faulty assumption that can be corrected, and by doing so the conflict removed. What do you think about it?"

"I don't buy it," Rick whispers to himself.

"Do you believe in win-win solutions?" Jim asks him.

"I guess so."

"So you do accept what Johnny just said."

Rick doesn't see the connection clearly, but now Johnny continues.

"Let's use our conflict to demonstrate how powerful this approach, called 'evaporating cloud,' is." And he moves back to the overhead projector.

"Let's expose some hidden assumptions," he says. "We claim that in order to control cost, managers must try to manage according to the cost world. Why? Because we assume that the only way to achieve good cost performance is through good local performance everywhere." As he speaks he adds the assumption to his diagram.

"And why do we claim that in order to protect throughput

managers must try to manage according to the throughput world? Because we assume that there is no way to achieve good throughput performance through good local performance everywhere." When he finishes adding it to the diagram, he pauses to give everyone time to digest.

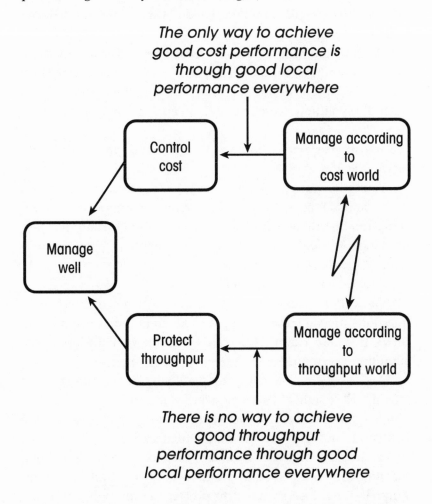

The only way to achieve good cost performance is through good local performance everywhere

Control cost

Manage according to cost world

Manage well

Protect throughput

Manage according to throughput world

There is no way to achieve good throughput performance through good local performance everywhere

"Where do we stand? We now have three alternatives. We can challenge the upper assumption, we can challenge the lower one, or we can continue to look for a compromise. What do you think we should do?"

Probably Johnny regards his question as rhetorical, because he continues to ask, "Who thinks that the upper assumption is wrong? That the assumption that the only way to achieve good cost performance is through good local performance every-where, is wrong? Please raise your hands."

About five people raise their hands. After a moment, a dozen or so join them.

"Don't be too hasty," Johnny warns them. "Those who think this assumption is wrong, do you know what you're claiming? You are actually claiming that most organizations, since the in-dustrial revolution, were wrong. Do you still want to raise your hand?"

Almost everyone who raised their hand before defiantly raises it again.

"Your prerogative," Johnny smiles. And then he continues, "Who thinks that the lower assumption is wrong? That the as-sumption that there is no way to achieve good throughput per-formance through good local performance everywhere, is wrong? Please raise your hands."

To Rick's astonishment, nobody does.

"The vote is clear," Johnny announces. "Unfortunately, such questions are not resolved by a democratic vote. We have to prove what we claim. How can we prove that the upper as-sumption is wrong?"

"And now we are going to see some fancy mathematical model," Rick sighs. "Wake me when it's over."

But Johnny doesn't use any mathematics. "You are still the bottleneck and you are the non-bottleneck." He points to his two volunteers. "The same scenario as before. We all agreed that the non-bottleneck should produce only ten units an hour. Why? Is it because we want to protect the throughput? Think about it.

"If the non-bottleneck will produce fifteen or even twenty, will it prevent the bottleneck from producing his ten?

"So why are we so adamant about restricting the non-bottleneck to only ten units an hour? Maybe the non-bottleneck is willing to answer?"

"Because if I produce more," Pullman confidently says, "the only result will be the accumulation of unneeded inventory."

"And if inventory goes up, what happens to cost?"

"Goes up."

"You see," Johnny addresses the audience, "we all asked the non-bottleneck to produce much less than he can, not in order to protect throughput, but in order to control cost. We instructed the non-bottleneck to restrict its local efficiency to only fifty percent, when it could achieve one hundred, for only one reason. To control cost. What does that tell us about our upper assumption?

"The only way to achieve good cost performance is through good local performance everywhere. Baloney!

Speaking slowly, stressing each word, he concludes, "We are chasing compromises, degrading our performance, making our life miserable, because of an assumption that is apparently wrong."

After a short while he repeats, "The only way to achieve good cost performance is through good local performance everywhere. The fact that so many managers and almost all our systems are based on this assumption is regarded by TOC as the current core problem of our organizations."

"I have to think about it," Rick promises himself.

"All the new management philosophies," Johnny is now on a roll, "implicitly recognized it. They all try to stress the importance of protecting throughput, they all try to shy away from local optimums.

"TQM and JIT are adamant about throughput even though they haven't realized that it mandates a much sharper focusing. Reengineering puts the emphasis on reexamining basic assumptions. A cornerstone of the learning organization is to replace unsatisfactory compromises with win-win solutions. Using the clarity provided by TOC and systematically using its analytical methods, all these philosophies, at last, merged into a coherent whole.

"But you didn't come here for a theoretical lecture. You want to see what can be done with it. In reality. What results can be achieved? In what time frame? And above all, how?

"What I'm going to do now is to share with you one of the most fascinating experiences I had last year. How, in UniCo, they turned around a losing company they bought. Turned it into a gold mine in just a little over three months. But my first hour is over and I was told to break for coffee. If you are still interested, be back in twenty minutes."

Chapter 12

I see that not all of you are back. Okay, I've learned my lesson. No more of that heavy, boring stuff. Instead, I'll tell you a story, everybody likes stories, about my most significant personal experience at UniCo.

One day I was called to the office of Don Pederson. He is a vice-president, but not like the other vice-presidents. Nobody reports to him, except for a few assistants. That doesn't mean that he is not important. At least for me he was very important. He is the one who signed my grant.

Anyway, until that day, my contact with him had been only through memos. I liked his memos. They were polite, short, and each one meant another trip. At that time I had been with UniCo for about six months, and it was the first time I was to meet him in person. I didn't have any problem finding his office; it's right next to the office of the CEO, which is supposed to mean something. Exactly what, I never found out.

Don is a very pleasant and open person. Surprisingly young. I doubt if he is much over thirty. But this guy taught me a lesson I'll never forget.

We had a lengthy conversation about the last place to which I had been assigned. It was a huge distribution center, and I showed him how they could optimize their truck schedules. According to my calculations, they could save at least fifty thousand a year. He showed a lot of interest, asked a lot of questions, and even looked at my elegant solution to a complex set of equations. I felt good. Here I am, the knowledgeable professor, teaching an executive how they should scientifically run their business.

I'm embarrassed to think about what he actually thought of me. A professor who spent a few weeks in a distribution center that turns more than half a billion dollars a year, and all he can come up with is a convoluted way to save, maybe, fifty thousand bucks.

But Don was polite. He said that it seemed they could use my talents. Then he told me how. They were about to acquire a new company, a steel mill; they expected to sign the documents next Friday. A month before, Don had devoted two days to do a brief analysis of that company. He suggested I fly there the next day, do an in-depth analysis, and prepare my recommendations. I liked it. I know a lot about the steel industry. I have published four articles about it.

I liked it a little less when he suggested he would meet me there the weekend after the company exchanged hands and we would compare notes. I was about to tell him my doubts, that a proper analysis couldn't be done in the ten days that were left, that you can't compare a riffraff analysis to a professional one, but I decided I'd better not. So I went.

They were waiting for me down there. I worked frantically. During the day I interviewed people, and nights I read tons of reports and tried to make some sense out of the piles of data I was accumulating.

At first I felt drowned. Slowly the picture started to unfold. The company, like many other steel mills, was losing money, hand over fist. But that's to be expected when competition is so fierce and steel prices are depressed.

The clients, when you dismiss their usual tendency to bitch and moan about their vendors, didn't have particularly bad complaints. Delivery lead times and due-date performance were comparable to the competition. So were prices, of course. Quality was slightly better, but not significantly.

Technology was good. Most equipment was state of the art. Except for the slitters, the machines that cut the plates to size. That equipment was bad, slow and wasteful. It must be replaced. I did the calculations. The payback was not much more than three years.

Inventory was a problem. Mountains of plates filled the company's huge yards. And it wasn't stored well; much of it was rusting. I spent a lot of time trying to find out what could be done. It wasn't easy because everybody was blaming everybody else. Finally, I found out that what they used for planning the work of that complex operation was an outdated computer system. Can you imagine? They invested a fortune in the furnaces, and another fortune in the rolling and coating departments, but they still used software written in the seventies. These steel people, I'll never understand them.

Raw materials were also a problem. Not the materials themselves, but the price they pay. They had to organize their purchasing differently. I spent a lot of time on it. I optimized the system. I was ready to show Don how, with three fewer people in the purchasing department, they could handle the same quantities and save a bundle. Minimum a million dollars a year, maybe even a million and a half.

On Friday they signed. I expected Don to arrive on Saturday morning. I was ready for him. But he called and said he had to finish something important and he would arrive on Sunday afternoon. I used the time to polish my calculations.

Sunday, at seven P.M., I was still in the lobby pretending to have tea, when he entered the hotel. He asked me to join him in his suite. I was eager to show Don my findings, to show off. So, I grabbed my papers from my room, decided that ten minutes was enough for him to freshen up, and knocked on his door.

He didn't want to look at my papers. His first question was, "What is the constraint of the company?"

I had spent enough time at UniCo to expect such a question. Naturally, I was ready. I handed him my list of constraints. Twenty-six of them. He glanced through the list, these executives read very fast, sighed, and put it aside. I wasn't surprised. With such a long list of problems, you would sigh too.

Then he asked me how much time, according to my analysis, it would take to bring this company to profitability. I didn't have an answer. Out of desperation I answered that it depended on what would happen to the price of steel in the market.

"Assume it stays at current prices," he said.

As far as I could tell, at current prices this company would never be profitable, but how can you say such a thing to someone who just bought it?

I remembered the joke about the person who committed himself to teach a dog to read in three years. He hoped that in three years the dog would die or the owner would die. Knowing how frequently steel prices oscillate, "In two years," I confidently said. Thank God he didn't ask me to justify it.

Rather, he asked how much money I thought had to be invested. For this I had a detailed, accurate answer. But once again he refused to look at the papers, he just wanted to know the bottom line. I hated it. But he was the one who signed my checks, so I told him: twenty-two million, three-hundred and forty thousand dollars. Approximately.

"I see," was his only comment. And then . . . And then he just said that the limo would pick us up at seven tomorrow morning, and accompanied me to the door.

Next morning they were waiting for us in a big meeting room. All the top managers, about twenty of them. We shook hands and then Don took over.

He told them that he didn't know much about the steel industry, and even less about their operation. And he asked them to help him to understand better because the more he knew, the less likely he would be to impose stupid decisions on them. He didn't leave any doubt that he was going to make some decisions.

Then he said that he had read all their financial reports, but that these reports did not tell him a thing about how they actually operate their company. He knew that for a long time "tons-per-hour" has been the prime operational measurement in the steel industry. And he asked them if they thought they were doing a good job monitoring tons-per-hour.

They thought they were. For about half an hour they explained, in detail, how they do it; on a work-center level, a departmental level and on a plant level. They explained how the data is gathered and processed. They presented the resulting reports and the graphs of tons-per-hour per shift, per day, per week, per month, per quarter, per year.

Throughout the explanation Don was very encouraging. When they were through, he agreed that there was no doubt that they were doing a thorough job monitoring tons-per-hour. He asked me for my opinion. I said I was impressed; that only now did I realize the meaning of a Prime measurement with a capital P.

Don was quiet for a while. And so was everybody else. At last he said that he was convinced that they were doing a good job monitoring tons-per-hour. What he was questioning was, should they?

For them it was heresy. In their world, the steel world, tons-per-hour is one of the pillars of their paradigm. It took them some time to digest that they are allowed to question it.

Don was flooded with reasons why they must monitor tons-per-hour. In my eyes, I must tell you, many of the suggested reasons sounded like "we must monitor it because we always monitored it." Don listened intently. He didn't interfere even when they started arguing among themselves.

Finally, when they calmed down, he reminded them that the main reason for an operational measurement is to induce the departments to do what is good for the company as a whole.

They had to agree.

At that stage, Johnny put up a transparency.

I know that it's difficult to read from the screen, so I'll read it, the same way that Don did.

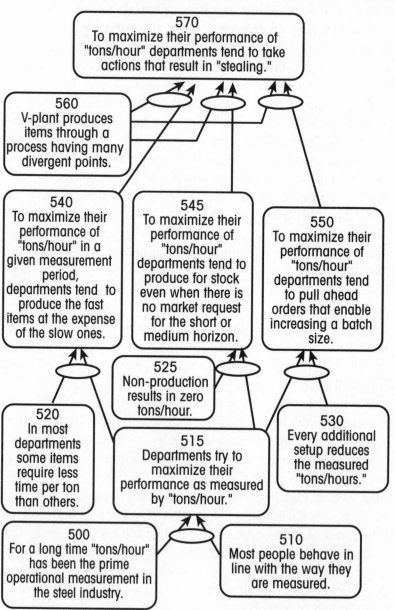

Don started from the bottom. In the steel industry, each department is judged according to how many tons they process per hour; the measurement of tons-per-hour is the prime operational measurement, statement 500.

He then quoted the famous phrase, "Tell me how you measure me and I'll tell you how I'll behave." He didn't have any problem getting agreement that most people behave in accordance with the way they are measured, 510. Then he reached the conclusion that in the steel industry, we are bound to find that departments try to maximize their performance as measured by tons-per-hour, 515.

Without hesitation, they confirmed it.

What does this lead to? On its own, it might make sense, but not when combined with other facts that exist in the industry. Like the fact that in almost all departments some items require less time per ton than others, 520. For example, in the rolling department, you squeeze red-hot steel into plates to produce ten tons of two-inch thick plates, which takes much less time than to produce ten tons of one-half-inch thick plates. The result must be that in order to maximize their performance of tons-per-hour in a given measurement period, departments tend to produce the fast items at the expense of the slow ones, 540. You can imagine what this leads to. High inventory of the fast items, while missing orders on the slow items.

They discussed it at length, debating the magnitude of the resulting damage. Some tried to minimize its significance. Don didn't argue. He didn't have to. The other managers did it for him. They brought up hard numbers to prove it. The numbers weren't funny at all. Everything was in the many millions. Actually, the accompaning anecdotes were very funny, if you have a twisted sense of humor like I do.

When that was settled, Don moved on to highlight that in the steel industry, significant setup times exist in every department. Twenty years ago a setup of twenty-four hours was common. Today, due to new technology, most setups are more in the range of three to five hours. Still significant.

Everybody knows that setup reduces the tons-per-hour. While you are doing the setup, you produce nothing, 530. Don asked them how long they would run after a four-hour setup. Minimum a whole shift and usually much longer, was the consensus. And if there are not enough orders? After these questions nobody argued with the conclusion: to maximize their measurement of tons-per-hour, departments tend to process orders ahead of time and out of sequence in order to increase the batch size, 550. Once again they discussed and tried to quantify the unavoidable results, the unnecessarily high inventories and unreliable due-date performance.

The worst situation for a department is to be idle. Non-production results in zero tons-per-hour, 525. It's no surprise that to maximize their tons-per-hour, departments tend to produce for stock, even when there is no market request on the short or medium horizon, 545. This definitely doesn't help the inventories.

At that stage I thought I finally understood why they have such mountains, and I mean mountains, of inventory. And why even though they promise that they will deliver a new order in seven weeks, they succeed in only about sixty percent of the cases. But I was wrong. The real killer was about to come.

What typifies the base industries, steel being one of them, is that the nature of their process is to have divergence of products at each stage of production. For example, in the rolling department, they produce many different plates from the same type of steel. Plates different in thickness. Once you produce a two-inch-thick plate, and later you change your mind and want to turn it into a one-inch plate, it's too late, the steel is already cold. It's the same in the slitting department, where they slit the plates to size. If you slit a plate to be seventy inches wide, you cannot later make it eighty inches. In short, in the steel industry, items are produced through a process having many divergent points, 560.

Now combine all this with each of the facts outlined in 540, 545 and 550, and what do you get? You get that to maximize their performance of tons-per-hour, departments tend to take actions that result in "stealing." No, nobody suspects that a worker puts five tons of steel in his pocket when he goes home. It's much worse.

For example, we prepare a specific plate for only two near-term orders; ten tons for sixty-inch-wide plates and another ten tons for seventy-inch-wide plates. The setup time in the slitting department is about three hours. To slit ten tons takes less. They try to run at least a full shift on the same setup. What happens? They slit all the twenty tons into one width and then scream hell that they were not given the material for the other order. You can imagine the resulting finger pointing, not to mention that on one hand we have a very unsatisfied client and on the other, plates with no demand.

Don guided them in making estimates of the resulting negative effects. They estimated the impact on lost sales, excess inventory, wasted cost, long delivery lead times, unreliable due-date performance, and, not less important, time wasted in heated quarrels between departments. The numbers were staggering.

Then, Don asked if they had any other problems. In the ensuing three hours I got a lesson in how to handle complaints. Don didn't dismiss anything they raised, even though some of them looked to me like pitiful excuses. With each problem they raised, Don made them quantify the negative impact. Then he guided a discussion of how much of that impact is due to what was already described on his diagram. He kept on referring to it as their current-reality-tree; the logical description of the effects stemming from the fact that they operate in the environment created by the tons-per-hour measurement.

It was amazing. For example, they complained about their vendors not always delivering on time. Don made them realize that if they did not produce so much excess inventory, they could hold much bigger stocks of raw materials. Vendors not delivering on time would then become a minor point.

Or, the problem that clients sometimes change their minds at the last moment. After inquiring, 'last moment' turned out to be four weeks before delivery. If lead times were much shorter, this also would not be a problem, as they would have delivered before the client had a chance to change his mind.

To make a long story short, they became convinced that all the other problems were either relatively insignificant or were significant because of the existing chaotic environment. There was a real, true consensus that the core problem, the constraint of the company, was the fact that their prime operational measurement was tons-per-hour.

Don pointed out to them that this was actually very good news. Yes, very good news, because all their competitors suffered from exactly the same core problem. Correcting it would give this company a tremendous advantage.

You're probably asking yourselves, like I did, how come the steel industry uses such a devastating measurement? The answer is that their systems, like every other industry, are based on the cost world. Remember the basic assumption of the cost world? The only way to achieve good cost performance is through good local performance everywhere. If you believe in that assumption you'll be forced to use a measurement like tons-per-hour.

Now you understand much better why TOC claims that currently the core problem of our organizations, the constraint, is the fact that so many of our management systems are based on the belief that the assumptions of the cost world are valid.

You can imagine how embarrassed I was remembering the list of twenty-six constraints I had handed to Don just the previous evening. Now I knew why he hadn't bothered to read it. Once you understand TOC you realize that there are no real-life systems with twenty constraints. Such systems will be chaotic to the extent that reality will have eliminated them a long time ago. Real-life systems have one, maximum two, constraints.

I also understood that I did not have the tools needed to enable me to identify the constraint. No wonder. That was the first time I'd ever seen a proper analysis, that I'd seen a current-reality-tree.

At the opening of my talk I said that in my eyes the most important contribution of TOC is the research methods it introduces. Now you understand why. The thinking process of TOC, called the evaporating cloud, caused a revolution in my work. This method, or better still, this thinking process, is the antithesis of what I was used to doing.

Presenting a problem as a conflict between two necessary conditions makes a lot of sense. But I was almost programmed to proceed to find a compromise. In academia we don't call it compromise, we call it optimize. Three-quarters of my articles are optimization models of some kind. You can imagine how difficult it was for me to accept that a much better solution, or even solutions, emerge by refusing to attempt to find a compromise, and instead concentrating on exposing the underlying assumptions.

The cause and effect thinking processes of TOC, one of which is the current-reality-tree, forced me to go through another paradigm shift. But after that experience with Don I was not about to continue fiddling with symptoms.

I had spent ten days interviewing everybody, just to reach the decisive conclusion that this operation would never be profitable, unless steel prices went up substantially. Along comes Don, and in one month, yes, one month, he made them profitable. A month later he dealt with the next constraint, their marketing policies. And today this same company has the same people, no worker was laid-off, no manager was replaced. And has the same equipment, not one piece of equipment was bought. This same steel company is now a gold mine.

Well, that's my story. And the time is up. So, if you have any questions . . .

They held him there for another hour.

Chapter 13

Most of the class is already sitting down, but to my surprise, there is almost nothing on my desk. I'm aggravated. These people are supposed to be serious. I gave them a homework assignment, they argued to get more time, I gave them two more weeks . . . and now only one report is submitted?

Something is wrong. Before I get all over them, I'd better find out why.

"The subject for today," I say in a calm voice, "is the magnitude of the safety people put into every step of a project. You were supposed to interview people and find out how much safety they add. And then you were supposed to submit your findings. Today."

They look at each other. They look at their desks. They look out the window. Nobody looks at me.

"It was impossible to find anything," Ted snaps.

"How come?" I'm genuinely surprised.

"Because people don't like to talk about the safety they put in."

"Did you push?"

"You bet I did," he says bitterly. "That was my mistake. All it did was irritate some foremen." Without a smile he adds, "And believe me, those people you don't want to irritate."

"Anybody else have better luck?"

Nobody answers.

"Charlie, did you find out anything?"

Smiling, Charlie replies, "I didn't get any threats, if that's what you mean, but I didn't get any real answers, either. People don't remember, or don't want to remember. In any event, nobody admits to putting safety in their time estimates. When I mentioned safety of two hundred percent, they laughed in my face."

"Of course they would," I say. "You two went about it all wrong. What was your mistake?"

"If I knew, I wouldn't have made it." Ted doesn't take criticism well.

And he is right. When I gave the assignment, I should have been more specific.

"There is no point asking people how much safety they put in because people believe that they give realistic estimations," I explain. "The problem is in what they call realistic. Remember Mark's reaction before we explained the probability distribution? Remember his astonishment when he realized how big the difference is between the median and eighty percent point?"

"So how were we supposed to do it?" Ted is very snappy. Probably his questions to the foremen stirred up a hornet's nest, and he still stings.

"You should have asked people for their opinion about the chance of finishing a task in the time they estimated," I answer.

"That's all?"

"Yes. We can do the translation. We know that an evaluation of eighty percent chance means about two hundred percent safety. Sometimes more. Remember what we said about the shape of the probability distribution: the higher the uncertainty, the higher the resulting safety."

"If that's all you wanted," Charlie says, "then I did find something."

"Let's hear it."

"From my inquiries, one thing came out very clearly." And he makes the following declaration: "The time estimates are impacted, in a major way, by the last overrun the programmer had."

Everybody is laughing. They too are aware of this phenomenon.

Then Charlie continues. "I don't think that there is much point in asking computer programmers to evaluate their chance of finishing on time. Computer programmers will never admit ninety percent chance, not even eighty, because a programmer who finished on time has not yet been born. At the same time, let me tell you, there is nobody like an experienced programmer to pad himself with safety."

Not knowing much about programming, I ask, "Why?"

"It's obvious. Otherwise they wouldn't have the time to add all the bells and whistles that nobody needs. If you don't sit on a programmer, he will never finish, he always has another something he must add."

Thanks to Charlie, the class mood is cheerful again. Even Ted is less gloomy.

"I didn't ask the right questions," he says. "But from my experience I can tell you what the answer will be."

"Yes?"

"Every foreman will say that if everything is ready for him, and that's a big if, then he won't have much difficulty finishing his share on time. They don't talk in terms of probabilities, but they mean over ninety percent."

Now that everybody understands what they were supposed to do, more share their experiences. Their experiences are amusing, but not leading us anywhere.

Not entirely happy, I ask the class, "Does anyone have anything more than just general impressions?"

"Yes," says Mark. "We did force people to give their evaluations. We even prepared a questionnaire for that. It's in our report. As you can see there, except for one person who is known to be paranoid, the vast majority said they think that they have better than an eighty percent chance of finishing on time."

"There is a caveat to it," Ruth adds. "Almost everybody emphasized that their answer is dependent on others not delaying them, and not being loaded with too many other things at the same time."

"That's reasonable," I say. "So, where do you think we stand?"

And I answer my own question. "I think that we did confirm what we said last time. We expected people to give estimates that would give a good chance of finishing their step on time, well over a fifty percent chance. And that's what you found. At the same time, we predicted that people would not realize how much safety this over fifty percent means, and you verified that as well. That basically sums up your findings."

"That's not all," Fred calmly says. "Mark, Ruth and I found something else. We found that five plus five equals thirteen."

"What?"

"It's very common," Mark comments.

"It's very common that five plus five equals thirteen," I repeat. "What kind of a joke is that?"

"Whenever a step in a project is a collection of several tasks, each done by a different person," Ruth explains, "the boss of this project asks each person for their own estimates, adds them up and then adds his own safety factor on top."

"So, if one estimates his task to take five days," Fred continues, "and the following task of the same team is estimated to take another five days, the person in charge will give an estimation of thirteen days."

"I see."

"That's standard," Ted confirms.

"Sometimes," Brian interjects, "there are several management levels involved. Each level adds safety."

This phenomenon is news to me. Considering human nature, it makes sense, but it doesn't appear in the textbooks I have read. "Is this the case at your companies as well?" I ask the class.

Many confirm it.

"There is something else," Fred adds. "In our environment, top management is frequently not happy with the final estimation of when a project is expected to be finished. They want the results sooner. So in half the cases, when all the estimates are done, they demand the lead time of the project be cut by, say, twenty percent. This global cut is usually translated into everyone, across the board, having to cut their times by twenty percent. By now everybody is used to it, so they inflate the final estimates by twenty-five percent to start with."

Many nod. It must be happening not just at Fred's company, but at others as well.

"Any more good news?"

There isn't any. "Let's see where we stand," I say. "As far as we can tell, there are three different mechanisms by which safety is inserted into the time estimates of almost every step of a project.

"The first one is that the time estimates are based on a pessimistic experience, the end of the distribution curve.

"The second is that the larger the number of management levels involved, the higher the total estimation, because each level adds its own safety factor.

"And the third is that the estimators also protect their estimations from a global cut.

"When you add it all up, safety must be the majority of the estimated time for a project."

Then I ask, "Do you see something strange?"

Charlie is quick to pick it up. "If our estimations include so much safety, how come so many projects do not finish on time?"

"Let's take a specific project, so we can really examine this question," I say. "Is anybody willing to present a case where a project was very late?"

"The Denver airport."

"I mean a project you were involved with. One where you know what really went on."

Ted raises his hand.

Jokingly I say, "Ted, admitting that you had a late project is contrary to the image construction companies try to promote."

He laughs, "We are among friends here. And I have a real case that shows that sometimes projects will be late and you can't do anything about it.

"A year ago, we built a new mall. A big one. We were late by two whole months. We blamed it on last-minute changes, but the truth is that we were struck by particularly bad weather. Also, you can't imagine how many things we had to redo. There was nothing we could do."

"How much time, in total, was lost?"

"About two months. That's why we were late."

"Maybe," I say. "But tell me, what was the original estimate, from start to finish of the whole project?"

"Fourteen months, I think."

"Ted, don't run away from the dilemma we are facing. If most of the time estimates are actually safety, your safety was much more than two months. You shouldn't have been late."

Ted does not agree. "The fact is we were late. I think the reason is that we build safety against regular problems. Somebody doesn't show up, a window is damaged, a bad weather day. That type of thing. We don't plan on major catastrophes."

"I don't buy it," Brian argues with him. "If I understood the probability distribution correctly, we do guard against big surprises. Otherwise, why do we claim that we take two hundred percent safety?"

"Then I don't believe that we take so much safety. At least in our company we don't."

Brian doesn't let him get away with such a statement.

"Ha! You are different. But if I'm not mistaken, you told us that in your company, people use estimates that put them in the range of ninety percent probability of finishing each step on time."

The debate between them might develop into something unmanageable. Especially with others trying to jump in. I decide to cut it short. "Well," I say, "is there something wrong in the logic that leads us to assume that so much safety exists? Or is there something fundamentally wrong in the way we are using that safety?"

There is nothing wrong in our logic, and they know it. Even Ted. But that doesn't help them to come up with an answer.

I turn to the board and draw two boxes. "Suppose these boxes represent two consecutive steps in a project. The estimated time for each step is ten days. Now suppose that the first step took twelve days. That means that the second step will start two days later than planned. That's obvious. But what will happen if the first step finishes in eight days?"

"Is it a trick question?" someone asks.

"If the first step finishes in eight days, when will the second step start?" I repeat my question.

A light is coming on in Ted's eyes. "It will start when it was originally planned to," he confidently states, and smiles.

"Why?"

"Because the team that finished ahead of time won't report it. You see, the way we are set up, there is no reward for finishing early, but there is, in fact, a big penalty." And he explains, "If you finish early you just invite pressure from management to cut the times. Your friends, in charge of other similar teams, will not like it, to say the least."

"So what will happen?"

"They will find ways to play with it. Don't worry, if they don't want you to find out that they finished, you won't."

As a second thought he adds, "Besides, even in the unlikely event that they do report it, it doesn't mean that the second step will immediately start. That team is probably busy doing something else, they might even be at another site."

"Another site, hmm . . ." Ted's explanation is tied too strongly to his specific environment, the construction industry. I'm afraid that my students won't see how general these phenomena are. That's why I ask, "Do we find this type of behavior in other industries?"

"Definitely," Charlie is firm. "Even though not exactly for the same reasons. A programmer is not afraid of his peer's reaction, but as I already mentioned, it will not cross his mind to say that he finished ahead of time. He or she will always find something in the program that can still be polished a little more."

"And if they report an early finish?" I encourage him to continue.

"Still not much will happen. The person who is supposed to do the next step knows that there is sufficient time, so what's the rush?"

"Let me see. What both of you are telling us is that it is likely that an early finish will not be reported. And even if it is, frequently the time gained will not be taken advantage of by the next step; it will just be wasted."

I write on the board: "A delay in one step is passed, in full, to the next step. An advance made in one step is usually wasted."

There were many other comments, but the conclusions held.

"You see what it means?" I try to drive home the message. "In sequential steps our deviations do not average out. Delays accumulate, while advances do not. This can explain how so much of our safety disappears."

I let them think about it a little, and then proceed. "What happens in the case of parallel steps?"

I draw four boxes all leading to one. "Suppose that in three of these steps we were early by five days. And in one step we were late by fifteen days. Statistically, if we average out all four boxes, we are on time."

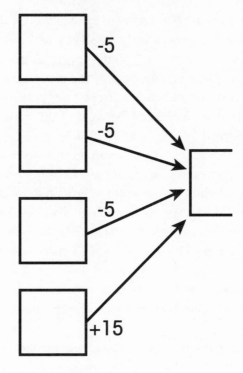

The class bursts out laughing.

"In the case of parallel steps, and in any project there are many of them, the biggest delay is passed on to the next step. All other early finishes do not count at all."

"What you are telling us," Ruth is thinking hard, "is that most of the safety we put in doesn't help at all."

"Correct."

"If we could find a way to put the safety only where it's needed . . ."

Ted can't control his impatience. Mockingly he says, "If we had a crystal ball that would tell us, in advance, exactly where the problems would occur, then . . . Come on Ruth, let's be realistic."

Ruth blushes a little, but she is not going to be bullied. "Still, let's face what we see here. The only thing that counts is the performance of the project as a whole. At the end, it doesn't matter how many steps were not completed on time, as long as the project was delivered when promised. And what do we do? We try to protect the performance of each step. Most of this protection is wasted. So even though we put in that much safety, the project as a whole is exposed."

Ruth's words trigger a train of thought in my head. "We try to protect the performance of each step." That sounds to me like a cost world mentality. "The only thing that counts is the performance of the project as a whole." That sounds much more like the throughput world mentality. Is it possible that we are facing here the conflict that Johnny Fisher was talking about? Is it possible that bad performance is the result of a wrong assumption? What assumptions have we made?

The class is silent for a long while.

I'm supposed to do my thinking outside class, here I'm supposed to teach. I break the silence. "Anybody want to comment on what Ruth said?"

Fred raises his hand. "There is something that bothers me from before. For the past half hour we've been speaking as if we agreed that people put a lot of safety into each step. I'm not sure about it. I've checked some numbers, and they don't support that conclusion."

That's interesting, especially coming from Fred. "Share it with us," I say.

"In our company we keep records of when each step started and when it was completed. I used the data to compute the elapsed time of the steps, and I compared it to the original estimates. Do you know what I found?"

He waits a second or two, then tells us. "I found some steps, very few, for which the elapsed time was shorter. Now I understand that it might be a result of people's reluctance to report an early finish. It also solves another problem that I had, estimations that are too accurate. Now I understand why almost half the steps were reported finishing almost exactly on the nose.

"What bothers me is what I found for almost a third of the steps. For this large group I found that the elapsed time was about ten to twenty percent longer than the original estimate. If there is so much safety in the original time estimates of each step, how can we explain it?"

And he continues. "Everything that I've heard so far can, maybe, explain why the safety does not protect the completion time of the project. The safety is wasted in the connection between one step and another. But what I'm talking about here is that I haven't found the safety that is supposed to protect the performance of each step."

"That's important," I say. "It means that if we don't have a mistake in our logic, it must be that we are somehow wasting the safety, not just on the project level but on the step level as well. Anybody have an idea?"

After a long while, Tom raises his hand. "Maybe we just waste it?"

I'm eager to encourage more students to speak up, so softly I say. "So it seems. Can you give an example?"

"Our assignment for today."

I don't see the connection. But Charlie does. "Tom is absolutely right."

For those who didn't get it yet, and that includes me, he explains. "When we got the homework assignment we all claimed that two weeks was not enough time to do it. And we succeeded in getting a postponement. Now how many of us, after we screamed that we needed more time, went back and immediately started working on the assignment? I bet that no one did."

Tom nods his head.

"The students' syndrome," Brian says. "First fight for safety time. When you get it, you have enough time, so why hurry. When do you sit down to do it? At the last minute. That's human nature."

Fred jumps on the bandwagon. "Only once we start the work can we find out if there is a problem or not. If there is, we start to work frantically. But we have already wasted the safety, so now we are going to be late. Yes. This can explain why, in spite of all the safety, so many steps finish a little late."

"Very good, Tom," I say. "It seems that everybody agrees with you. Based on personal experience, me too."

"I hate to spoil the party," Mark says in his deep voice, "but I don't agree. What Tom says exists, but not always. And definitely not when we are under pressure."

Then he adds, "I went over the steps Fred checked. I can tell you that in many cases that he checked, people were working under pressure. For example, many of the steps that took longer than estimated were done in the digital processing department. That department has been under constant pressure for years. Believe me, they don't waste time."

I look at my watch. Only ten minute left. If I want to finish this topic I'll have to speed things up.

"Mark," I say, "this digital processing department. Are they involved in many projects?"

"All projects. That's our bottleneck. We can't afford to dedicate these people to one project at a time. And in each project, there are many steps that they must be involved in."

"So, if I understand you correctly," I say, "each person is multi-tasking."

"You understood correctly."

"In that environment, being under pressure means that many people are putting pressure on them to work on different things? I suspect that the digital processing people are in no position to really know which tasks are more urgent?"

"How can they," Mark agrees. "I think that their priority system is according to who shouts loudest. And every project has several people who know how to shout."

"So what do they do?"

"The best they can. Jumping from one project to the other, trying to satisfy everybody."

"Typical multi-tasking," I say. "Do you all realize what impact multi-tasking has on lead time?"

They apparently don't.

"Suppose that a person has three steps to do, A, B and C. These steps might belong to different projects or the same project, it doesn't matter. Each step takes ten straight working days. If our person works sequentially, the lead time of each step is ten days. Ten days after he starts B, for example, B is released for somebody else to continue the work. But our person is under pressure and he tries to satisfy everybody. As a result, he works on a step for only five days before he moves to another step. Suppose that the resulting sequence is A, B, C, A, B, C. What is the lead time of each one of the steps?"

I draw the diagrams, so it's easier for them to figure out the answer.

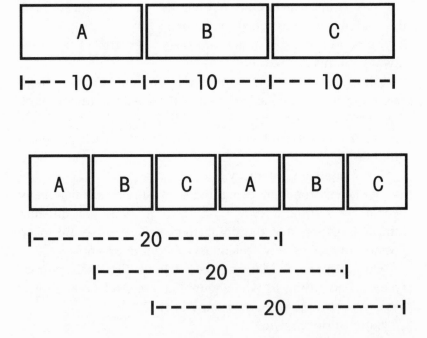

Mark is the one who gives the answer. In astonishment he says, "The lead time of each step doubles. I knew that multi-tasking was bad, but I didn't imagine to what extent. And we didn't even consider the setup time that is wasted."

"Multi-tasking is probably the biggest killer of lead time," I say. "And we all suffer from it. Call it meetings, call it emergencies, call it other jobs. The impact is the same. Lead time inflates. If you think about it, whenever you give a time estimate you know that the actual time is just a fraction of your estimate, but you intuitively factor in the impact of multi-tasking."

This matches their experience, because they all agree.

"Wait a minute," says Mark. "There is something wrong here. In our company, we have to come out with a new product every six months or so. Therefore, if we increase all the safety times, we increase the lead time of all projects. That means that more projects will be going on at the same time."

I don't see his problem. "Correct, but what's your problem?" I ask.

Slowly, he continues. "More projects means multi-tasking. And according to what we said, it means that lead times will lengthen. So what you are telling us is that if we add more safety time it won't help because the lead times will become longer?"

"Self-fulfilling prophesy," Ruth says. "You claim that it will take you longer, it will. And we all know it. My problem is different. How come we allow multi-tasking?"

"Isn't it obvious," I answer. "Without multi-tasking we might run into times where people don't have enough work. Efficiencies will go down."

"Who cares about local efficiencies." It's the first time I've seen Fred get excited. "Isn't the only important thing to guarantee that the projects will be successful."

Mark joins in. "And on the bottleneck, with multi-tasking or without it, we'll have enough work."

More join in. I know where it's coming from. Johnny Fisher is teaching them the course in production. I'd better not step into that mine field. Not without preparation.

I raise my hand to stop the attack. "Hold your horses. Wait a minute." When they quiet down, I continue. "You are raising very interesting ideas. But look at your watches. It will have to wait until next time."

That stops them.

"Let's summarize what we found today." They all start writing. "We found three mechanisms to put safety in. Now it seems that we also found three mechanisms to waste that safety. One we called the student syndrome, there is no rush so start at the last minute. The second is multi-tasking. The third involves the dependencies between steps; these dependencies cause delays to accumulate and advances to be wasted.

"Which brings us to your next assignment. This time it's simple, so I don't expect any misunderstanding. I want you to submit an example for each of the three mechanisms that people use to add safety, and for each of the three mechanisms people use to waste the safety. The examples should be taken from your reality and must, I repeat, must be numerical."

Chapter 14

I'm waiting to go into the dean's office. This meeting is a formality, and in general, I hate formalities, but not this one. This one took me over nine years to reach.

Two weeks ago, the last committee approved me for tenure. Finally. Now the dean has to sign, and then the president. They are rubber stamps. Our dean has a custom of meeting with every approved candidate personally. To show interest, to give a pep talk, to . . . I don't know what. So here I am, with my best tie on.

I'm shown in. Dean Christopher Page II shakes my hand and guides me to a chair. It's the first time I've been in this office, but I've heard a lot about it. Thick carpet, beautifully framed paintings. Not exactly my taste, but here they fit. Nice furniture. Not just nice, comfortable.

Then I notice that he isn't smiling. That's not like him.

"I'm afraid I have bad news for you," I hear him say. The rest comes to me as if through a fog.

"The business school is not going to give tenure for a while. . . . Not to anybody, no exceptions."

"Yes, I know what a good teacher you are."

"What can we do? It's the global strategy."

"Jim Wilson talked to me, but you must understand, it's not in my hands."

"Sorry, but no. There will be no extensions. Not even for one year."

"The president is absolutely firm. I'm afraid it's final."

"All I can do is give you a very good reference letter. You deserve it."

Thanks a lot.

I don't see anybody as I go back to my office. Strange, but only one thought keeps booming in my head, "Will Judith leave me?"

I lock my door, sit at my desk, and try to assess my situation. I'm too upset.

Two hours later I reach for the phone and call Phil, an old buddy. We studied together. He has tenure at a private college, where the pay is much better. I must explore the alternatives.

"Phil, is there an opening at your college?"

"Sure there is. But Rick, you should have applied five years ago, when I begged you to."

"Forget the past. What do I have to do to apply now?"

"It won't help," comes the discouraging answer.

"What do you mean 'it won't help'? Do you have an opening or not?"

"Of course we have. The pressure here is immense. But Rick, listen to me. They are not hiring people like you anymore. The market is full of people who teach business."

"I'm a very good teacher."

"I know, but Rick, that's not the point. Today they either hire full professors for the image, or adjunct professors. And for those they only take people with years of field experience. You don't stand a chance."

No, I don't. Three more phone calls, to friends in state and community colleges, clarifies it for me. I missed the train. I'm thrown out of academia with no way back. And for what? I still don't understand it.

Maybe Judith is right. Maybe it's time for me to make some money, to go into the consulting business.

Consulting for me is almost equal to prostitution. But maybe I'm just affected by people who didn't dare go out in the real world. People who prefer producing worthless articles to being judged by tangible results. I bring myself to flip through my address book once again.

"Hi, Daniel. Do you need more excellent people?"

"Like whom? Like me."

"I'm flattered. So what is my next step? When should I fly to meet with the partner in charge?"

"Send a resume, uh-huh . . . highlighting my consulting assignments? But, Daniel, I never consulted."

"I see. Grants that I solicited? Listen, Daniel, I think that you have it all wrong."

Five minutes later, smarter and furious, I put down the phone. The greedy bastards.

Since I've already started, I decide to go all the way. I call smaller partnerships. Then small ones.

It's ridiculous. I'm supposed to get my own clients. I'm supposed to do everything alone, and on top of that to pay fifteen hundred dollars a month for office and accounting services.

Forget consulting, I tell myself, I'm not cut out for it anyway. I can't sell myself. I don't like to, and I don't know how. Besides, teaching is my life.

So what is the alternative? A high school teacher. And what am I going to teach in high school?

Forget alternatives, I say to myself. I'm not giving up on teaching students. Think. There must be something that can be done. They can't throw me out like this. I've delivered on my end of the bargain, there must be a way to force them to honor their end.

I stand up and go to Jim.

One glance is enough for him. "So you heard the news. Sorry

Rick. I was trying to get ahold of you. Left you messages everywhere."

"I know," I say, and drop into a chair. "I thought that you
were looking for me for the draft of the next article."

He doesn't say a word. Just looks at me sympathetically.

"Jim, I'm not going to lie down and let them do this to me."

"You never will, but what can you do?"

"I don't know. That's what I came to ask. I'm determined to
fight. What are my options?"

"Options?" he repeats. "There aren't many. I wonder if there
are any."

"There must be. You know the system, you must know a
way."

He thinks for a while, then starts to talk, "You don't have a
problem with the business school, here we are all for you. You
passed all the committees, and I didn't hear even one bad comment."

"So, what is the problem?"

"It's B.J. That's what makes it so tough. You see, B.J. decided
to put a freeze on all new financial commitments of the business
school. Of course the first one is granting tenure. I didn't know
about it, but the dean has been fighting with her for months. It
got to the point where B.J. threatened that if the business school
submits any candidates for tenure, she will not only reject them,
but she will demand a big budget cut."

"So you are telling me that I'm being sacrificed for some po-
litical fight? That all I worked for is going down the tube because of some . . . some power struggle."

He nods. "So it seems."

"Somehow I have to reach B.J.," I say. "She is the key."

"That's easy," he surprises me. "According to the university
rules, you can demand a meeting, and she must see you. But
how can it help? Everybody knows what a cold-blooded efficiency machine she is. The only thing she cares about is the
university."

"I'm counting on it. Thank you, Jim," I say, and leave him a little puzzled.

I know that I contribute, so there must be a way to show it to her. I just have to find that way.

Now, only three days later, I'm in B.J.'s office. She has given me a whole speech about the trends in the MBA market. As if I care. I realize what a stone wall I really face when she brutally says, "Sorry, but when you make an omelet, eggs must be broken."

So now I'm an egg. And a broken egg, no less.

Finally, I realize that there is no chance of bringing her around to see it from my side. I have to talk her language.

"What happens if I can bring more students into the executive MBA program?"

This stops her short. She thinks about it, and then, not particularly interested, asks, "How do you plan to do it?"

I don't have a plan yet, but I also don't have anything to lose.

"I'm teaching the project management course. Projects are where the big money is."

She doesn't respond. I take it as a sign to continue.

"It might come as a surprise to you, but the state of knowledge in this field is appalling. Almost no project finishes on time, or budget. And if they do, it's because the original scope has been compromised."

She signals me to continue.

"We have made major progress. Teaching how to substantially better manage projects is of tremendous value to any industry."

"Any organization," she agrees.

Encouraged, I charge on. "This know-how is so valuable that I think I will be able to convince companies to send managers to learn it."

I definitely have piqued her interest. "Tell me more," she says.

So I tell her. I tell her about the dilemma of early start and late start, the dilemma that jeopardizes the ability to focus. I tell her about the progress measurement that jeopardizes real progress. Then I tell her about the safety we so generously insert into each step and then so carelessly waste. I talk for almost an hour. She listens. She even asks questions. I'm impressed with her ability to grasp these concepts so quickly.

Then she says, "You talked about the problems. Do you have solutions?"

When she hears my response, her interest takes a nose dive. I'm about to lose it all. Desperately, I say, "I think I can find the answers. And I can bring ten more people to the executive MBA program." It doesn't seem to work.

I try to apply to her business sense. "Their tuition will more than cover my salary," I say as convincingly as I can.

"Professor Silver," she softly says, "ten additional students will not be enough. Tenure is forever, and there is no guarantee that you will be able to pull off such a miracle a second time. That is, if you can pull it off at all."

I try to object. She cuts me off. "What you told me is interesting. We must provide valuable knowledge. I believe that otherwise there is no long-term future for an MBA program. In my opinion, in the business school we don't currently teach much of value. I keep hearing about the first year shock, the shock our graduates get when they leave school and start work, and then find out that almost everything we have taught them simply doesn't apply.

"So you don't have to persuade me that it's important to teach a better way to manage projects. The question is, are you the person to do it?"

"Try me. I'll deliver."

Where I got this confidence from, I don't know. Maybe it came out of my desperation. B.J. probably thinks so as well, because she says, "Such things take much longer. And I have a policy to follow."

"I can do it."

She gives me a long evaluating look. "Are you practical

enough? Because if not, how can you develop practical solutions to such problems?"

I'm trying to find something to answer, when she says, "Tell you what. Words are nice, but I need proof. Prove that you are practical by bringing ten more students to the executive MBA program, and I'll extend you another year."

I tried to argue, but it was like talking to the wall. I went out disgusted with the university and with myself. In academia one is supposed to be judged by his ability to teach and his ability to research, not his ability to sell the university to students. I deserve to get tenure. That was the verdict of the professional committees, and now I've become a salesman, and for what?

Chapter 15

We are gathered in a small classroom; Jim, Johnny, Charlene and myself.

It's gray outside, and cold. Not just outside, inside as well. My mind is not on this meeting. It's not anywhere else, either. For the past few days I haven't seen any point in pulling myself together. I just go through the motions. I show up every morning, I teach, I stare at some academic journals, and I go home. I don't even have the heart to break the devastating news to Judith. It's not right, but what's the rush? What can she do about it? Having the satisfaction that she was right all along is small consolation. I know I don't have the right to hide it from her. We'll have to return the Blazer. We'll have to sell the house. Probably we'll have to move. Where to? Doesn't matter. It's gray outside, and cold.

"In my systems layout course," Jim says, explaining the purpose of the meeting, "I started hearing very insightful comments from the students. Sometimes so insightful that I didn't know how to handle them. Charlene has been complaining for a while that the students have been giving her a hard time in her cost accounting course. Now Rick has started to encounter the same thing in project management.

At first we didn't know where it was coming from, but after your colloquium, Johnny, we don't have any doubt."

Smiling, Johnny reacts, "So you want me to stop teaching what I'm teaching?"

"Not at all," Charlene is quick to respond. "I think what you teach is very good. Every professional in accounting has known for a long time that something was wrong. True, your students irritate me a little with their new ability to point out the fallacies so clearly. But I don't have a real problem with it. I just want to know more about it than they do. Is that too much to ask?"

"That's basically what we all want." Jim puts his hand on Johnny's shoulder. "Your colloquium was fascinating, but it wasn't enough. We want to know more about what you teach in your production course."

Laughing, Charlene adds, "First, because we do want to know. Second, because we can't afford not to know."

I don't say a word. I don't agree. I, for one, don't want to know. What does it help to know? I'm through with stuffing my head with all this garbage. It won't help keep the house for Judith. It won't help me keep Judith.

Besides, all this mumbo jumbo about links in a chain. The mistake there is so obvious, even a child can spot it. So much fuss about nothing.

"I'd be delighted to," Johnny is all smiles.

Of course he is delighted. Why shouldn't he be? He is a chaired professor.

And I'm sure that last year, on his sabbatical, besides his majestic salary from the university, UniCo paid him another fortune.

"The production application of TOC," Johnny is all business, "is a straight deduction of the five focusing steps." He stands up and goes to the board. "The first step, as you may recall, is identify the constraint." And in capital letters he writes '1. IDENTIFY.'

"Suppose you identified the constraint, the bottleneck. Then the next . . ."

He is so full of himself I can't stand it any longer. I cut him off. "Okay, let's cut the crap and for a change let's be practical," I challenge him. "In practice there is more than one constraint. And don't tell me that one work center has to be loaded more than others. In mathematics it might be so, but in reality the differences are negligible."

I ignore the surprised expressions on Jim's and Charlene's faces, and charge on. "It's clear even in your chain analogy. Theoretically one link is the weakest. But practically? In a real chain, the next weakest link is almost the same, it's just infinitesimally stronger. All your arguments are based on nothing."

I've shown them what I really think about their theories. I'm not going to continue being the nice guy. In the time I still have left in academia I'm going to speak my mind. When something is garbage, I'm going to call it garbage.

The way Johnny continues raises my blood pressure. With his best scholastic manners he has the nerve to say, "This is a very interesting question."

Interesting, my ass. I nailed him, and he knows it.

Not surprisingly, he immediately starts to cover up, to cloud the issue with fancy mathematics.

I barely listen when he mumbles something about when you use linear programming to solve the equations, and then you use sensitivity analysis, you see that a system having two constraints results in only unstable solutions.

Jim starts to take my side. "Johnny, can you answer Rick's question without using mathematics?"

"Sure," he says.

Leaning forward, I challenge him, "Let's see." I'm not going to let him get away with some empty convoluted sentences. I've played this game long enough. Enough to know how to expose phonies.

On the left-hand corner of the board Johnny draws a line of circles. "These represent work centers. The flow of material is from left to right."

Let it be.

"Let's suppose that we want to utilize this work center to one hundred percent," and he puts a big "X" on one of the middle circles. "We can't do it unless the previous work centers constantly supply enough material."

"Don't forget that in practice, machines are not working smoothly," I'm making sure that he doesn't turn it into one of those artificial examples Johnny likes so much to use in his articles. "And don't assume any neat pattern. A worker may slow down, tools can break, materials jam. You never know; you only know that it happens."

Johnny smiles at me. "Precisely." He behaves as if I'm trying to help him. "Under the realistic conditions that Rick so vividly described, how can we guarantee that our X machine will always have enough material so that it will be able to work constantly?"

"Put enough stock in front of it," Jim collaborates.

"Good idea." And Johnny draws, in front the circle with the X, a hump that is supposed to represent a pile of stock. "Now, as Rick told us, Murphy hits; one of the work centers upstream has a problem. The flow of material to the X machine stops. But not to worry, due to Jim's suggestion there's a pile of material ready. We can continue to utilize our X machine to one hundred percent."

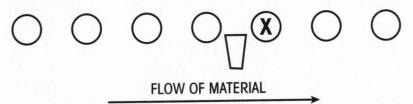

FLOW OF MATERIAL

Eliyahu M. Goldratt

I like it. It's simple. And Johnny will soon admit that he is wrong. There is no problem having as many bottlenecks as we want, the only price is some inventory. I'm not going to let him give a baloney speech on the cost of holding inventory as an excuse for having just one bottleneck. Oh, no.

"So far, so good," he smiles. "But what, unavoidably, happens during this time? The flow of material to X stops and X continues to work, pulling from its pile. The amount of inventory in the pile must go down."

Johnny stops, turns to me and asks, "Should we agree that Murphy does not strike only once? That sooner or later one of the feeding machines will, once again, stop?"

Even though I see where he is leading, I must agree.

"And if so, from time to time, the pile will continue to be drained. Can we afford to let the initial pile be drained to zero?"

I don't answer. I don't like people asking trivial questions. I hate it even more when they bother to answer their own trivial questions. Which Johnny does. "If we do, the next time Murphy hits one of the feeding machines, our X machine will be starved, it won't work for one hundred percent of its time. So, if we don't want this initial pile to be drained to zero, when the problem in the feeding machines was corrected and the flow resumed, what did we have to do?"

"Rebuild the pile in front of X," Jim plays Johnny's trivial question and answer game.

"But to do that," Johnny says triumphantly, "the feeding machines have not only to supply the ongoing rate of X, at the same time they also have to rebuild the stock. Quickly, before Murphy hits again. Which means . . ." he looks directly at me, "which means that each one of them must have more capacity than X."

He goes back to his seat. "Conclusion. If we want to utilize even one resource to one hundred percent, all its feeding work centers have to have more capacity. Since Murphy is not negligible, and the feeding machines have limited time to rebuild the stock, they must have more than infinitesimal excess capacity. QED."

I stare at the board. Johnny's proof is surprisingly elegant. I can't find any crack in it. But if he is right on this point, I have to accept the resulting five focusing steps.

So what? What's bad about it?

In the background I hear Jim asking, "How much excess capacity do the feeding work centers need to have?"

And Johnny answers, "It depends on the magnitude of the breakdowns, not less on the frequency of the breakdowns, and, of course, the amount of the stock you allow or want to build in front of X."

I know what's bad about it. Since the minute I heard it the first time, I knew that these five focusing steps are the key to solving all the riddles of project management, and I wanted to try and give it a shot. But now, now that B.J. puts it as a condition to prove myself worthy of tenure, I'm not willing to degrade myself by playing her game. I've already proven myself, I passed all the professional committees.

Jim and Johnny are now both at the board writing some equations.

But what if I can beat her at her own game? Not a chance.

Why do I take for granted that it's beyond me to solve the projects' problems?

"Rick?" Charlene touches my arm. "I need to know this stuff. Do you mind letting Johnny continue?"

I stare blankly at her.

"In two hours I have a class to teach, and you are wasting our time now."

She is so self-centered. I need to know this stuff even more than she does.

"Why are you picking on me?" I say.

She doesn't answer. Instead she turns back to them. "So, the first step is 'identify.' Johnny, Jim, can we proceed?"

"And the next steps," I say, "are 'exploit,' then 'subordinate,' then 'elevate' and 'go back.' That's simple. My question is, how do I convert it into a logistical solution? Something practical."

Jim returns to his seat. Johnny wipes their scribbles from the board and writes the remaining four steps.

When he finishes, he turns around, and half seriously, half sarcastically he asks me, "Can I use an analogy?"

"Why not?"

He turns back to the board and adds legs and noses to the circles. "Now they are a troop of soldiers on a march. Do you see the analogy to a plant?"

We don't.

"The first row of soldiers is walking on virgin road, processing raw material. Each row in turn processes the same piece of road until the last row releases the finished goods, the part of the road the troop, as a whole, has left behind."

Raw
Materials   FLOW OF MATERIAL ————————▶   Finished
                                                                          Goods

"Now I see," says Charlene. "It's slightly confusing at first because in a plant the machines are fixed and material is moving, here it's the opposite. But I agree, it doesn't matter."

"If the first row consumes raw materials," Johnny continues, "and the last row releases finished goods, the distance between the first and last rows is work-in-process inventory. In this analogy we can see the inventory visually."

I'm not interested in inventory, it's not a factor in projects. "What about lead time?" I ask.

"It's the same," Johnny answers. "Production lead time is the time elapsed from the minute the first soldier stepped on a particular point until the last soldier stepped on the same point. So, the bigger the distance between the first row and the last row, the longer the lead time. Work-in-process inventory and lead time are twin brothers."

I don't have a problem with it, I just want him to talk in terms of lead time rather than inventory.

"When the troop leaves the camp," Johnny continues to explain, "the soldiers are packed together. But when we look at the same troop two miles down the road, what do we see? They are spread all over the countryside."

"Lead time has gone through the roof," I comment to myself.

"The officer will stop the troop, regroup the soldiers and then they'll continue. Stopping the troop means that throughput has been lost. We see that even in this simple 'plant' there are problems. On average, lead time is too long, and from time to time throughput is lost."

I start to like Johnny's analogy.

He turns to Charlene. "What happens if we use efficiencies to judge the performance of each soldier?"

It's an interesting question. How does one go about answering it?

Charlene goes about it systematically. Slowly she says, "Being efficient means doing more in a given time period. In our analogy, it translates into 'walk faster.' "

Picking up speed she continues, "That's exactly what we want. We want the soldiers to move faster. I do not see any problem."

Neither do I.

"Do we want every soldier to move faster?" Johnny asks her, "or do we want the troop as a whole to move faster?"

"What's the difference?"

"You're forgetting that we have a bottleneck," and he points to the solider bearing the big X. "The rate at which the troop as a whole moves is dictated by the rate of the bottleneck. Our X fellow is not the first soldier. If we encourage each soldier to walk as fast as he can, the troop will spread. Lead time will go up."

Yes. We all knew it, but it's so easy to fall into the trap of the cost world.

"It's like what you've shown us about the steel mill," Charlene remarks, "measuring each work center by tons-per-hour."

"Precisely," Johnny nods. "The question is what to do instead? Look at that analogy, it might give you a clue."

We look. It doesn't.

"How can we prevent the spreading?" Johnny is not giving up on us.

Still not knowing the answer, I try to joke, "We can tie the soldiers to each other, with chains."

"That's the assembly line," Jim jumps up and starts to pace. "That's the conveyor belts of the assembly line."

I think about it for a second. "I don't get it," I admit.

"Me neither," says Jim, and sits down again.

Johnny draws chains between his funny soldiers. "What is the effect of putting chains?

"Look at the soldier before the bottleneck. By definition that soldier is faster than the bottleneck. So the chain between them is tight. Now this soldier can no longer move at his own pace; due to the chain, he is restricted to moving at the pace of the bottleneck. Spreading is prevented. Jim is right, an assembly line is a case where we use chains. The limited space of the conveyor belt serves as a chain. Look at it.

"Suppose that in an assembly line one work center is faster than the work center downstream from it. The conveyer belt between them will be full of products, the chain is tight. If that conveyor belt is full, our fast work center cannot continue to produce at it's own rate. It is forced to continue producing at the rate at which space becomes available on the conveyor belt. Which means, producing at the pace of the downstream work center."

"The same is true for Just-In-Time," Jim is saying slowly. "JIT doesn't use conveyor belts, it uses containers, of which a limited number are allowed to accumulate between work centers. It's exactly the same concept."

"Correct," Johnny agrees. "And we all know how effective assembly lines, or JIT are. Lead time under those methods is by far shorter than what we see in conventional production.

"So, what is the essence of these methods?" He continues to ask, "Why do they work so well?" And then answers, "All they've done is to put a cap on the amount of inventory they allow to accumulate between each two centers. Once the local inventory reaches its cap, the work center generating it is not allowed to continue producing at one hundred percent of its capability."

I understand, but something doesn't fit.

"Please wait," I ask him. "I'm trying to put my thoughts in order. Otherwise I don't have a chance of transferring what you are showing us in production to the project environment. Bear with me."

"Take your time."

"I'll tell you what bothers me," I say after a short pause. "In your colloquium you presented what I consider to be a generic process of five steps. If I followed you correctly, you claimed and proved that following these steps is not only beneficial, it's mandatory."

"Correct," Jim answers for Johnny.

"In my vocabulary, 'mandatory' means that if you don't do it, good results will not occur."

I'm stuck. I cannot put my finger on what bothers me. Jim continues for me, "Now we see methods, the assembly line and JIT, that do work. Which means that either they follow the five steps or the five steps are wrong."

Thank you, Jim. Now I know how to continue. "It's apparent that assembly lines and JIT do not follow the five steps. Not only don't they start with identifying the bottleneck, they are not even considering the existence of a bottleneck at all. So where is the mistake in the five steps?"

Johnny looks at us, then at the board. Then he sits down.

"I don't follow you," Charlene says to Jim. "You talk as if it's all or nothing. What happens if JIT follows just one step? Won't it yield better results than a method that doesn't follow any?"

"It will," I agree. "But which of the five steps does JIT follow? It's apparent that it doesn't obey the first or second."

"What about the third?" she asks. "It forces work centers to work at less than their maximum local efficiency. It does force subordination."

"Yes, it does," I once again agree with her. "But then . . ." Something is still wrong.

"But then," Johnny continues my trend of thoughts, "then, if we follow all five steps, not just one, we are bound to get a better method. And that's exactly what we get."

"Wait," I stop them again. "This is important, so can we please take it a little slower? Before you show us a better method, which now I'm convinced must exist, let's see if we can spot, in JIT or assembly line, something that is not satisfactory."

"Why is that important for you?" Jim is curious.

"He just wants to find out," Johnny explains for me, "if, without our knowledge of the five focusing steps, we could have predicted that a better method exists."

"Actually," I clarify, a little embarrassed, "I haven't gone that far. I just want to check if the problems that I've identified in projects also exist in assembly lines."

Charlene looks at her watch, but Jim and Johnny encourage me to give it a try.

I don't know how.

I stand up, go to the board and slowly pick up the chalk. I look at Johnny's soldiers, all tied together now with chains. "As we said, the chains actually symbolize a restriction on the amount of inventory allowed to be accumulated locally," I say. Johnny already drew a hump of inventory in front of the X soldier. Mindlessly I add humps between each two soldiers.

"Johnny," Jim says, "can't we regard these humps as queues before machines?"

"That's exactly what they are."

"Let's not talk inventory," I impatiently say. "Let's talk time."

"Go ahead." Johnny is very patient.

"If this work center has a problem," I point arbitrarily to one of the soldiers, "then the hump represents the time that the next soldier can still work before he will have to stop. In a way," I slowly say, "these humps represent the protection a work center has. Protection against problems occurring upstream."

"You could say so," Johnny agrees. "They represent safety."

"Safety. Safety. You are right. Here is the connection to projects, don't you see?" Y-E-S! "I told you that we have to relate to inventory as representing time. In production we protect a work center with inventory, in projects we protect a step with safety time."

"I see what you mean," Jim comments, "and I agree. Still I think that there is a difference. In projects the situation is worse."

"Why?"

"Because, if there is a stoppage, inventory does not disappear. In projects, time is gone, forever."

I'm still thinking about it when Charlene comes from left field with "I have a problem with all of that. Why do we do that? Why do we try to protect the performance of each work center? I thought that we already agreed that local efficiencies don't count."

Somehow these sentences sound familiar to me. Then I recall that Ruth's complaint was "We try to protect the performance of each step." I also recall what Ruth said next. "We put in so much safety, and the project as a whole is still exposed." Does it mean here that the performance of the assembly line is exposed? Of course.

"Thank you, Charlene."

"What for?" She is still irritated by my rudeness.

"You showed me the problem with the assembly line, or JIT. We spread the protection everywhere and it's not enough, the line as a whole is exposed. In an assembly line one work center goes down and very quickly it stops the whole line."

"Of course" she says. "The only place that we want one hundred percent efficiency, the only place that needs protection, is the bottleneck. Exactly as Johnny showed us at the beginning, that's where the pile of inventory should be, right before the bottleneck, nowhere else."

I agree, but I don't see how to do it. We have to build the protection there, nowhere else. But at the same time we must prevent the spreading. It seems contradictory.

We are all looking at Johnny.

It takes some time before he realizes that we are waiting for him to show us the solution, the better method.

"But you solved it," he says, surprised.

Jim speaks for all of us, "If we did, we haven't noticed."

"You already said it all. The starting point is the bottleneck. To exploit it we must protect it against disruptions everywhere else in the process. That's why we must make sure that a pile of inventory will be built in front of it. But not a mountain, that will cause inventory, or lead time, to go too high. So . . ."

He stops talking, waiting for us to continue.

We look at each other. "So, we don't know how to do it," I say.

"Tie the first soldier with a rope to the slowest soldier, to the bottleneck. That's all. What's the point in tying all the soldiers to each other? It will only force inventory between them rather than allowing the inventory to flow toward the bottleneck and accumulate there. Of course, the length of the rope, we call it the buffer, will dictate how much inventory in total you allow."

I'm trying to digest.

Jim does the same, but aloud. "If we tie the first soldier to the bottleneck, then the first row will be forced to walk at the rate of the bottleneck. That's good, spreading of the troop is prevented. All the other soldiers, being faster than the bottleneck, will jam pack, some behind the first row, the others behind the bottleneck. So the troop will spread over a distance that will be almost equal to the length of the rope we choose. That's neat. It will also guarantee that there is a gap before the bottleneck, so if one of the upstream soldiers stops, the bottleneck can still proceed. The inventory, the safety, accumulates there. Very nice, Johnny."

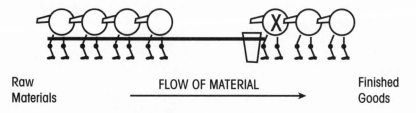

Raw Materials   FLOW OF MATERIAL   Finished Goods

"In practice," Johnny continues, "what we do is the following. First you identify the bottleneck. Then you choose the length of the buffer. Usually a good rule of thumb is to take the current production lead time and cut it in half. Then, you . . ."

So even in production they measure the buffer, the protection, in terms of time. What Johnny is talking about now is not too important for me. In projects, not like in production, the work is done only once. I will not be able to copy the mechanism from production, but I can transfer the concepts and find the appropriate mechanism. I have the key, I just have to follow the five steps.

I can already see the main questions I'll have to figure out the answers for. What is the bottleneck in projects? We have to tie the rope to something. How does one choose the buffer?

But I already see so many answers. Tying the rope will give the answer to the early start versus late start dilemma. It will also restrict the amount of work that is released, and therefore the problem of multi-tasking will be considerably reduced. I'll have to think much more about it, but I feel that the answers are around the corner.

Charlene stands up. "I'm sorry, but I have a class to teach. Johnny, there is something else I want to ask you. Local efficiencies and variances are wrong measurements. I fully accept. But what are the alternatives? What should we measure? Or do you suggest not using any operational measurements?"

"Not at all," he is quick to deny. "Do you want to schedule another meeting to discuss it?"

We all take out our diaries.

Chapter 16

"So far, does it make sense?" I ask them.

I can see how Mark, Ruth and even Fred are ready to jump down the throat of anybody who does not agree. Luckily, there are no targets.

The extent to which these three have become zealots is surprising. Their turnaround happened last session, when I guided the class to develop the solution. Not that they were dragging their feet before, but now it's like they have seen the light; they behave as if all their future depends on implementing it.

Tuesday morning all three came to my office and stepped all over each other trying to convince me to come to Genemodem and talk to Mark's team.

"The solution is almost against human nature," Mark was quite desperate. "I don't know how to persuade people to strip away their safety."

"And group consensus is vital," Ruth added.

Fred continuously repeated, "If the team doesn't buy in, results will not follow."

They didn't have to press so hard; I would give my left arm for the opportunity to try our ideas on a real project.

Now it's Thursday, and for the last three hours I've been talking to the team assigned to the development of the A226 modem. I don't know a thing about modems, nevertheless, I have succeeded in convincing them that I do know a lot about the pitfalls of managing a project. It wasn't easy, but I was able to get a true consensus on the current situation. It's written on the board.

1. We are accustomed to believing that the only way to protect the whole is through protecting the completion date of each step.

As a result,

2. We pad each step with a lot of safety time.

3. We are suffering from three mechanisms which, when combined, waste most of the safety time: a: student syndrome, b: multi-tasking and c: delays accumulate and advances do not.

We also agreed, and that was much easier, on what does make sense: the five focusing steps are also written on the board.

The real challenge is still ahead. Can I convince them to adopt the logical derivative of all that's written on the board? Can I lead them to develop the solution?

I take a deep breath and dive in.

"So what is the constraint of a project? What should we choose as the equivalent to the bottleneck?"

No answer.

Since they are interested in the subject, such silence can mean only one thing. I asked a question that demands too big a leap. I'll have to slice it into smaller chunks.

"Okay. What I'm asking you now is to ignore the pile of problems that you currently face and imagine the following scenario. You developed an excellent product, the A226 has been released on time and marketing turned it into a big success. Where is the constraint of the company?"

"In production," one answers.

"For sure," another backs him up. "With our best products, production never succeeds in adequately supplying the initial market demand."

"So in our futuristic scenario, there probably will be a bottleneck in production. What is a bottleneck?" And I answer my own question, "a bottleneck is a resource with capacity that is not sufficient to produce the quantities that the market demands. In this way the bottleneck prevents the company from making more money."

They don't have a problem with that.

"Let's go back to the situation as it now stands. The A226 is in your court, in engineering. What now prevents Genemodem from making more money from A226?"

"We haven't finished developing it yet."

"Exactly," I say. "So, in engineering, the desired performance is not quantity but? . . ."

"Finishing the development on time." They don't have any problem answering.

Mark is not entirely happy. "Or before time," he must interject.

We are in the team's room; there must be a PERT chart of their project somewhere. I locate it hanging on the opposite wall. It's big and colorful. I cross the room and stand beside it.

"Look on this chart," I ask them. "It represents all that has to be done to develop your modem. What dictates the lead time from start to finish of this project?"

"The critical path," they immediately answer.

"So what is the constraint of a project? What should we choose as the equivalent to the bottleneck?" I repeat.

"The critical path."

It is as simple as that. Why did it take me a whole week of floundering until I found the answer? Probably because the obvious is sometimes the last thing we see.

"Fine," I say. "We identified the constraint. What do we have to do to exploit it?"

"Don't waste it."

I fooled myself long enough on answers that look good but are meaningless. What's the meaning of "don't waste the critical path?"

It doesn't have any meaning until you express it in different words, and that's what I have to squeeze out of them. I had a hard time doing just that with my class; now I'm much better prepared.

"Don't waste what?" I ask.

We go through the expected questions and answers. The answers move from "critical path" to "time" and then, when we once again clarify that the time is based on estimates and pressures, we finally arrive at: "Don't waste the time allotted for the critical path." Any waste here will delay the project.

Semantics? Maybe. But semantics are sometimes crucial.

Now I ask the big question. "How do we, currently, waste the time allotted for the critical path?"

Based on the last three hours, they now have a lot of answers. Too many answers. But they seem to go out of their way to avoid the obvious one. Nobody mentions the core problem, the fact that we pad each step with a lot of safety time.

Maybe it's because of their fear of letting go of their precious local safeties, maybe they just don't see it. I don't know. I only know that I have to spend quite a lot of time relating each answer back to what is written on the board. Pointing out, over and over again, that it won't help us to deal with symptoms, we must deal with the core problem. We must bite the bullet and deal with our tendency to pad each step with a lot of safety time.

Maybe it was so difficult because of the implied action: "So, you want us to reduce the time to one-third?"

"I don't want you to do a thing," I clarify. "I just point out the unavoidable conclusions stemming from what you said. Do you agree that we shouldn't protect each individual step with safety time?"

"Yes."

"Do you agree that each step has a minimum two hundred percent safety?"

After more beating around the bush, the answer is still, "Yes."

"One plus one is two."

I had to repeat it, in one form or another, at least five times. At last someone asks, "But are we going to put in some safety?"

"Of course," I say. "Murphy does exist. But we are going to put the safety where it's going to help us the most. We are going to put it so it will protect the constraint. What is our constraint?"

"The critical path."

"So we have to protect the completion date of the critical path? Correct?"

"Yes."

"We put all the safety at the end of the critical path. Stripping the time estimates of each step frees up sufficient time to create a 'project buffer.'" I draw two pictures to clarify what I just said. The original critical path and the critical path with the project buffer. That helps.

Step #1	#2	#3	#4

They start to translate it into what it means for their project. The A226 has to be ready six months from now. There are many steps on the critical path that are not done yet. Their current estimates lead them to believe that they will be late by two months, which in their environment is verging on a crime. They already talked about saving time by compromising on some of the performance of the modem, but Mark hasn't allowed it yet.

"If we take the current estimates for the remaining steps," I help them, "it adds up to eight months. If we do what we just said, we can create a project buffer of more than five months!"

Nobody likes it. Not Mark, who booms that a five-month buffer is much too much. And not his people, who categorically state that anyone who thinks they can finish their individual tasks in one third of the time must be out of their mind.

For a while, it's a zoo.

Mark has to use his voice at full volume to quiet them down.

"With these trimmed estimates," he tries to calm them down, "I understand that for each individual step, the chance of finishing is only fifty percent."

There is rapid response. "Fifty percent, ha!" "Less than ten percent." "Not a chance."

It's one thing to agree that theoretically there is more than two hundred percent safety. It's another thing to commit to a trimmed estimate. Inertia.

"I'm not going . . ." Mark's voice booms above everybody else. "I'm not going to put anyone to the wall if he or she doesn't finish on time.

All I want to see is that we are working on it as fast and as prudently as we can."

It helps. Especially when he repeats and repeats and clarifies what he means.

Some caution against creating such a buffer. "Top management will immediately trim it."

"Not a chance," Mark is confident. "The project is well on its way. Top management is not going to mess with it now. We just have to deliver on, or before, the original promised date."

At last they settle on the following. The time allotted for each step will only be cut by one-half (Mark squeezes from them some lip service that they will try to beat these times). On the other end, the project buffer will not be equal to what they trimmed. It will be set to only half of it. Mark is adamant that two months is more than enough. I suspect that he insisted on it in order to put the project back on the promised date.

I add their version to the diagrams on the board.

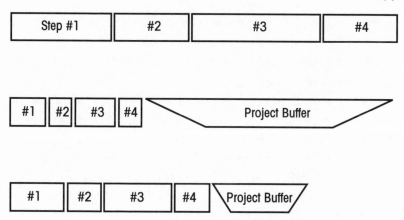

When all this is settled, Mark passes the baton back to me.

"Exploit the constraint," I start. "Don't lose any time on the critical path. We really can't do a good job of exploiting the constraint until we do the next step, until we subordinate everything else to it."

"Why?" Ruth asks.

"Without subordination," I answer, "we are unable to protect the constraint from losing time due to problems occurring elsewhere."

She agrees. The others look puzzled.

I explain. "So far you've dealt with the steps of the critical path itself. That will surely help. But tell me, hasn't it already happened in this project that you suffered a delay on the critical path because of a problem that occurred outside the critical path, in one of the many feeding paths?"

They laugh and start to bombard me with examples. I don't understand their jargon, but I let them speak. It's important that they realize that most problems that impact the critical path do not occur on the critical path itself. That's the only way they'll realize that subordination is not a nicety, it's a must.

When they somewhat run out of steam, I ask, "Do you agree that we must do something about it? That somehow we must protect the constraint from problems occurring at the noncon-straints?"

They don't have any problem agreeing. Their problem is fig-uring out how to do it.

"What is done in production?" I ask. "How do they protect the bottleneck from problems occurring at the nonbottle-necks?"

"They build a buffer of inventory before the bottleneck."

"We don't talk in terms of inventory," I remind them. "We talk in terms of time. So what do we have to do?"

"We have to build a buffer of time."

"Where do we have to build these time buffers?" I go to the PERT chart hanging on the wall and put a ruler on the critical path. "What is the meaning of 'before the bottleneck' in our environment?"

It doesn't take them long to conclude that we must insert a time buffer at the points where a feeding path merges with the critical path.

"Where are we going to take the time from?"

By now they have the formula. For each feeding path they decide to cut the original time estimates of the steps in half and use half of the trimmed lead time as a 'feeding buffer.'

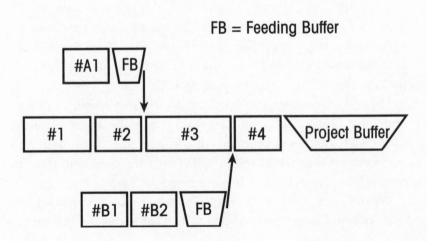

FB = Feeding Buffer

In less than half-an-hour we have a new PERT chart. It's amazing how much the computer software available today simplifies clerical work. It's also amazing to what extent this sophisticated software doesn't help us solve the real problems.

They examine the result. The situation looks much better than one might expect. Only in two feeding paths have delays already swallowed the buffer that we just created.

"I told you that it wouldn't work," one skinny guy is quick to conclude.

"What do we do about it?" Mark asks me.

"Concentrate on bringing them back on track," I answer. "But I don't see any reason for alarm. In each of these two cases the delay is about two weeks. Don't forget, if you really can't get it back on track, you still have a project buffer of two months."

That's an angle they hadn't thought about yet. The 'feeding buffer' protects the critical path from delays occurring in the corresponding noncritical paths. But when the problem causes a delay bigger than the feeding buffer, the project completion date is still protected by the 'project buffer.'

They like it. My attention is now on something else. On each of the two paths that are very late, the step that they are working on now is marked in red. This red color probably indicates top priority. My problem is that there are many other steps that are red.

I point to one red step where, according to their numbers, the buffer it feeds is still untouched. "What is the urgency in finishing this step?" I ask.

Nobody answers. Mark moves closer to examine what is written on the red step. He turns to one of his people. "Why the urgency?"

"I don't know," this person answers, and points to our skinny guy.

"You see the next step?" He has a matching squeaky voice. "My people are supposed to do it."

"So?"

"And they can't start before that step is finished."

I still don't get it.

Mark doesn't either.

"You know that they finished everything else," comes the squeaky explanation.

They are all over him. The efficiency syndrome is alive and kicking, not just in production. I wonder how many of their 'emergencies' are such false alarms. They probably wonder the same because they check every red dot on their chart. In the end, only four remain.

It's much better, but we still haven't finished.

"There is something else that might delay the critical path," I remind them. "Sometimes everything is ready for a step on the critical path except for the appropriate resource, which is still busy doing something else."

We discuss how to prevent such delays. They invent the resource buffer.

That's a concept I haven't yet covered in class, and their debate teaches me a lot about the practical aspects of exactly how to implement it. But I can't stay any longer. It's our theater night, and I'm not going to let Judith down.

I leave. They are deep in the details.

Chapter 17

"It's much easier to implement than we hoped," Mark says, concluding his presentation to the class.

"Any results?" Brian asks.

Mark fidgets. "It's only four weeks since we learned in class what to do, and it's three weeks since we actually implemented it. Now, you know that in a development project of two years . . ."

"Three weeks is nothing," Brian completes Mark's sentence.

"I know. Still, can you see any tangible results?"

"What do you mean by tangible results?" Ruth is slightly snappy. "Do you expect that in three weeks we'll complete the project? I hope not. But then, what else would you call tangible?"

"Hey, I'm not criticizing," Brian defends himself. "I think that what you've done is terrific. I just wonder if you have any hard evidence of real progress. That's all."

Fred puts his hand on Ruth's arm, and to Brian, he says. "There are some numbers. But first I have to explain something.

Remember the criticisms we all had on the way we measure the progress of a project?"

"Yes. Vividly."

"Well, we changed the way we measure progress. Progress for us is now measured only on the critical path; what percent of the critical path we have already completed. That's all we care about."

"We are doing the same," Brian replies. "It does work much better."

So my students are using what they learn here. That's delightful news to me.

Fred nods and continues, "According to this measurement we have made a lot of progress in the last three weeks. For example, in the previous three months . . ."

"Forget the numbers," Mark interrupts. "Let me tell you what progress we made in much more real terms. Do you know what happens when it's clear to everybody that we are going to be late on delivering? Really late?"

In a bitter tone he answers his own question. "Everybody is then on the project leader's back to cut corners. First to compromise on the quality checks, then to trim targeted performance."

"Same thing in computer software," Charlie is all smiles. "No difference."

"A month ago," Mark is waving his big hands, "everyone on my team had already come to me with suggestions of which specifications to trim. They were all over me to start discussing it with my boss. Today, after only three weeks, this pressure is off. Brian, do you understand what this means?"

"They've started to believe that they can finish on time. Now that's impressive."

"Too good to be true," Ted speaks up for the first time. "I've listened carefully to what you've done, and all I have heard is that you moved some numbers around. How can it have such an impact?"

Not like Mark and Ruth, Fred is smiling. "Moving some numbers around may have a big impact. Ted, suppose that some numbers are moved from your paycheck to somebody else's. Will it have an impact?"

Ted joins the laughter. Then he clarifies, "Mark, I understand all of that, but there must be something more. What actually are you doing differently?"

"Nothing." Then, as an afterthought, he adds, "But you have to realize that the whole attitude has changed. As I already stressed, there are no more false alarms. People don't put pressure on others just because their people do not have enough to do."

Ruth steps forward. "There is another big difference. We don't have milestones anymore. It's not like it was before, when you knew you were supposed to complete your step in two weeks, so what's the rush. Now, it's different. Either you don't start a step, because it's too early, or, if a path is clear to be worked on, you work on it as fast as you can. You see, we trimmed the times to the extent that people are not sure anymore that they can finish the step on time. They don't dare procrastinate. I would say that the 'student syndrome' basically disappeared. Don't you think so, Mark?"

"Yes, of course. You see, Ted? Before, when we used milestones, and you knew that you had two weeks to complete a step, the two weeks were yours. I, as project leader, couldn't do much to push you to finish earlier. Moreover, if I came after one week and started to press, even inquired, you would have reacted as if I were out of line. 'There is still a week to go, what do you want?'

"Now it's different. We trimmed the times. Now people know that there is a fair chance that they will not finish the step on time. They fully understand why I'm concerned, why I came early to find out where they stand."

"That's makes sense," Ted concludes. "That will have an impact." Then he confesses, "I must say that only now do I see the human behavior aspect. I understood why we should trim the time estimate from a ninety percent chance of completing on-time to only a fifty percent chance, but only now do I see the full ramifications. In retrospect, it's obvious."

"If you do what makes sense," Ruth comments, "you find out that it makes sense from many other aspects as well."

Mark is not ready yet to dive into philosophical remarks. "There is something else that should be mentioned. Multi-tasking. Eliminating the false alarm and actually shrinking the time it takes to perform a step contributed a lot to the reduction of multi-tasking. People do not jump so frequently from task to task. There is much less nervousness. How much does it contribute to the shrinkage of the lead time? I don't know, but it must be substantial."

Ruth turns to me. "Professor Silver, you visit us every week. What is your impression?"

I can only talk about what I have seen, and you can't see much in one-hour visits. "I'm in no position to evaluate by how much multi-tasking has declined. One thing is clear, though. People are more focused."

"The project is much more focused, that's for sure," Mark confirms.

"May I say something?" Fred rhetorically asks Mark. "I think that one of the major things we did was putting the resource buffer in place."

"Yes," Mark says. "Previously it was very common for everything to be ready for a step, but the people wouldn't be. They were busy working on something else. We decided that this would never happen for the steps on the critical path. Now, on the critical path, when everything else is ready we must make sure, in advance, that the resources will be ready."

"How do you do that?" Ted is surprised. "This idea of resource buffer was the only thing out of what we said that I thought was totally impractical. Do you actually force a resource to do nothing one week before it's supposed to work on the critical path? And people go along with it?"

"No. We don't do it that way. A week before the expected time we just remind people that their work on the critical path is coming. Then three days ahead we give another reminder. And then again, one day before, when we know for sure that everything else is going to be ready. The important thing is that people know that when the time comes they must drop everything and work on the critical path."

"I haven't heard anybody complaining," Ruth says. "On the contrary, they appreciate the early warnings."

"This is very important," Fred emphasizes. "Without it I'm sure that most of the advances we have made would have been wasted. To show you how well we are doing, let me give you one number. Three weeks ago, when we started, the project buffer was nine weeks. Now it is still nine weeks."

"In spite of the fact," Mark adds, "that everyone thought that the times we left for each step were much too short."

"Thank you," I say. The class applauds.

As the three head back to their seats, Fred turns, "There is one thing I wanted to ask."

"Go ahead."

"I'm not happy with the way we measure the progress."

That stops Mark. "What's the problem?"

"I am monitoring just the critical path, and so far everything is fine. But I'm afraid that a problem might be brewing in a noncritical path, and by the time it reaches the stage that it delays the critical path, it will be too late."

"That's a problem." Mark is stuck in the aisle.

"Sit down," I say. "There is no problem. You are monitoring correctly."

I'm confident. In the last meeting we had with Johnny to discuss operational measurements we covered buffer management in detail. I'm convinced that what they are doing is okay.

"Fred," I say, "you are monitoring the project buffer, correct?"

"Yes."

"How?"

"It's very simple," Fred says. "If a step on the critical path is completed, for example, two days earlier than estimated, I enlarge the project buffer by two days. If it's late, I reduce the buffer. Actually I don't wait for a step to be completed. Every day the people who work on the critical path give me their estimates."

"Estimates of the percent of the work they finished?"

"No, I'm not interested in that. They give me their estimate of how many days until they are going to pass the hot potato to the next step. I must say that sometimes it looks funny. For example, last week the report from day to day was four days to pass the potato; three days; six days, they ran into a problem and they panicked. Then, next morning, it's down to one day. By solving the problem, they found a good shortcut."

"If you are afraid of a problem brewing in one of the noncritical paths, why don't you do the same thing there?"

He looks puzzled.

"Don't we do it?" Ruth looks confused. "Mark, how do you determine if you have an emergency on a noncritical path? Don't you calculate the same for each of the feeding buffers?"

"Come to think about it, basically we do. But not formally. Fred, can you monitor all the buffers, not just the project buffer?"

"No problem. I'll give you a daily report." Fred is very collaborative.

"How should they arrange such a report?" I ask the class.

"According to importance," one person answers.

"Define importance."

It doesn't take long for the class to create the priority list. Highest in importance are steps that reduce the project buffer, either because they are somewhat late and are on the critical path, or because although they are not on the critical path they are late to the extent that they have already swallowed the corresponding feeding buffer and then some.

Then they debate how to arrange the second category—the steps that are not yet affecting the project buffer but are consuming part of the corresponding feeding buffer. There are several suggestions.

Some claim that the only thing that makes sense is the accumulated delay, or in other words, the number of days already consumed from the corresponding buffer.

Others say that this number doesn't tell us much unless it is compared to the original length of the buffer. Ten days out of a buffer of thirty days, they claim, is much less of a problem than consuming five days out of a buffer of six. This group advocates percentage, the percent currently consumed of the corresponding buffer.

A third group, led by Ted and therefore very vocal, claims that none of the above is really important. The only thing that matters is how many days are still left in the buffer.

Personally, I don't think that it makes much difference. As long as they continuously monitor all the buffers, they will be focused. Arranging it in one way or another is not so important in my eyes. In any case, the list is relatively short. It doesn't contain the steps that are not yet supposed to be worked on, or the steps that have already passed the baton.

But it's a lively debate. Everybody is involved, even students who hadn't yet opened their mouths. So I let it go for a while. A long while. Almost to the end of the session.

It was invigorating until . . . until Roger spoiled it for me. I thought that this person came to class just because he finds sleeping in a chair more comfortable than his bed. Probably the heated debate woke him up.

When I finally summarized the three options on the board, he commented, "It will never work. No one will collaborate."

I had to really lean on him to clarify his statement.

"In my company," he pompously said, "I'm in charge of negotiations with the subcontractors. They will never agree to cut their lead time. They will never agree to report, definitely not on a daily basis. You know, you get something when you get it. Every prediction they give you, they themselves don't believe in. Like everything else that we study here, it's good in class, but reality is very different."

I started to argue with him, but he cut me off. "If you want, come with me to one of my subcontractors and talk to him."

I was furious enough to accept the challenge.

I know that it's nonsense. He will never arrange for such a meeting. But it's a pity that this excellent session finished on such a lousy note.

I'm gathering my papers when Brian approaches me. "I've already talked with the plant manager and the project leader. They are very interested in what we are learning here. You see, our project to expand the plant is in trouble."

He wants me to come to their plant. We talk some more. I gladly agree to spend a day with their team.

Lately my mood resembles a roller coaster.

Puffing, I stop in front of the arrivals monitor and check for Judith's flight. I'm trying to catch my breath. Where is it? Thank God, it's late. It will not land for another twenty-five minutes. I knew there was no need to rush. A little bit of snow and flights from Chicago are late. Gate 12.

Near the gate, there are no empty seats. It's jam-packed with passengers waiting to depart. I go to a nearby gate and sit down. I can hear the announcement from here as well. And if not, Judith knows to look around for me. It won't be the first time that I forgot myself in a book. The problem is that I don't have a book. I look around, somebody must have left a newspaper. Only the arts section. Oh, well.

Three aisles away a tall woman unloads her garment bag onto a chair. Good figure. She turns around to sit. It's B.J.

My first inclination is to cover myself with the newspaper. Too childish. Too late. She recognizes me. I smile, stand up and walk over to her. I can almost see the Rolodex flipping in her head.

"Good evening, Richard." She shakes my hand. "Any progress on bringing ten more students to our Executive MBA program?"

I was wrong. It's not a Rolodex, it's a whole data base.

I try hard to ignore the sarcasm I think I heard in her soft voice. "Yes, plenty," I hear myself answer.

Why do I have to exaggerate? Why do I feel compelled to show off? But I did make progress. Plenty.

"I think I found a good solution and we are already testing it. On an important project."

"How nice." She sits down.

She is not what one might call excited. I sense that she doesn't believe me. No wonder. A month ago I had a pack of riddles. Now, I claim I have solved them all. It is unbelievable. Can I explain that it's all because I was lucky to be handed such a wonderful foundation from Johnny? No. That would sound even more farfetched.

I'm still standing. She doesn't encourage me to sit. I have to talk her language. It worked before.

"I have a good chance to try it in more places. Once I get results," I promise her, "I'll start to talk with management about sending more of their people."

"And when will that be?"

"Two, three months from now. I hope."

"Good luck." And she opens her briefcase and takes out a book.

"You don't think I stand a chance, do you?"

She gives me a long look. "Professor Silver. Do you know what it takes to persuade a company to send a person to our program?"

Since I don't know, I wait for her to tell me.

"The person must press for it, and the company must be interested in him or her, interested enough to yield to this pressure. You are going about it all wrong. It's not the company that you have to persuade. Companies rarely initiate sending students. It's the people, the mid-level managers, that you have to entice."

"So you think that nothing will come out of my work with industry? I should drop it?"

I'm desperate, but not half as much as I am when I hear her

answer. "Not at all. The university always encourages community service."

Community service! I'm so provoked that I forget myself, and bitterly say, "And I thought you meant it when you said that you are interested in us giving valuable know-how to business!"

"Yes, I am." And she opens her book.

"Then extend my term for one more year."

She looks back at me and coldly, so coldly, she answers, "I have a policy, and we have a deal."

"Rick! Hey, honey." I look around. Judith waves at me.

"I have to go," I say.

"Yes. You have to go," she firmly replies.

Chapter 18

I enter the classroom. Charlene is still there, arranging her papers and talking to Fred.

I sometimes wonder if giving my course after an accounting class is a plus or a minus. It's a minus because in the beginning the students have a glassy look and it takes time to get them going. On the other hand, I think it's a big plus because whatever you do, the students are going to give you good reviews.

Charlene notices that I'm there. "Can I have a word with you?" She grabs my arm and drags me outside.

"Yes, sure," I pointlessly say.

"Will it be okay if I sit in on your class?"

Two months ago I was in no position to disagree; Charlene sits on the school committee for tenure. Now I don't have to be the nice guy anymore, but what's the point in being rude?

"Be my guest," I say, still wondering why she wants to do it.

"Thank you." And then she explains. "I'm still trying to digest what we heard from Johnny. I mean the 'cost world' and the 'throughput world.' Neither are new to management accounting, but . . . but in the existing know-how it's somehow convoluted."

"I don't mind you sitting in on my course, but how is it going to help you?"

"Management accounting deals with decisions and control. You, Jim and Johnny, in your courses, are dealing with the same issues, but from different aspects. So, I decided that in order to straighten out my confusion, I must invest the time, sit in on all your courses, and deepen my understanding."

I want to ask some more questions but I have a class to teach. We go back in.

Nothing is on my table. No wonder. Last time I was so irritated I forgot to give them a homework assignment. Now I don't have a smooth entry into today's topic. No big deal, I'll just jump into it.

"There are two types of projects," I start to talk. They start to write. "A project that is done by vendors and subcontractors, like the plant expansion project that Brian is involved with, and a project that is done mainly by resources of the company itself, like the product development project that Mark is leading.

"We heard from Mark how they implemented our ideas in their environment. Conceptually they have made many changes. Practically it boils down to three. If you recall, the main changes were: One. Persuading the various resources to cut their lead time estimates; Two. Eliminating milestones or, in other words, eliminating completion due dates for individual steps, and Three. Frequent reporting of expected completion times."

They write as fast as they can, but I was talking too fast, and they ask me to repeat the three changes. I do, and then continue.

"As we heard, it was surprisingly easy to implement these changes . . ."

"Whoa!" Mark booms.

Ruth backs him up, "If it weren't for you, explaining everything to our people, persuading them to collaborate. . . . I don't think that such a paradigm shift can be imposed."

"I fully agree," Fred supports his team members.

"Thank you," I say. "Persuading people to collaborate is always necessary. The time when you could dictate is over. If you want people to think, to take initiative, you cannot dictate."

They all nod.

"But the fact is that you did implement it in about one week. Mark?"

"About."

"My question is, how can we do it in the other type of project environment, where most of the resources are vendors and subcontractors? Roger, whose job is dealing with them, told us it's impossible. That they will never collaborate. Roger do you still think so?"

"Yes." And being Roger, he must add, "And whatever you say will not change it." He puts his head in his palm and shuts his eyes. I ignore him.

"Are subcontractors and vendors a problem? Did you ever see a project that was significantly delayed because a vendor or subcontractor was late?"

If there ever was a rhetorical question, that's it.

"It is also a problem for us," Mark comments. "We are less dependent on subcontractors, but delays from our vendors are a major problem."

I nod to him and continue. "So, the lead times of our subcontractors and vendors should be of tremendous importance for our projects. Nevertheless, how do we choose them?"

"They can tell you whatever they want," Ted is almost shouting. "But the truth is, it's price. My company is a subcontractor. So I know. They may talk about reliability and quality, but when they come to sign, it's price."

Ted doesn't have to shout. Everybody agrees.

"Price is important," I say. "But lead time is not less important. Sometimes more. That's where the change should start. We must understand the financial impact of a delay. We must understand that a three months' delay sometimes costs us more than giving another ten percent to all our vendors."

Some are nodding, most look skeptical. Brian doesn't seem to agree, and he is not the only one. I have to demonstrate my claim. Otherwise they'll think that I'm just exaggerating in order to make a point.

"Brian, two weeks ago you invited me to spend a day with the team responsible for the expansion project of your plant. The plant manager was there, the project leader and all his key people. They are all concerned that the project will not be finished on time. Can you tell the class a little bit about this project?"

"Sure." Turning to the class, he says, "It's a six-million-dollar expansion project. For us it is big. And it looks like it will be at least four months late. If we are late, let me tell you, some people will be bent out of shape. That's for sure. So, yes, everybody is very concerned. Wouldn't you be?"

I keep on asking, "Do you think that they know the penalty of not finishing this project on time? I mean the damage to the company?" Before he has a chance to dig himself a hole, I continue, "You are a major player on this team. Do you know the damage?"

"Sure," he says. Then, expecting I will ask for the answer, he corrects himself. "If you mean the dollar and cents impact, no I don't."

"What data do we need in order to answer this question?" I ask the class.

For a while nobody answers. Then Brian himself hesitantly says, "Expected sales?"

"Is this an answer or a question?"

"More of a question," he admits.

"But you do know the answer. Let me guide you. We invest in a project in order to get something that will bring us benefits."

"Of course."

"Therefore, it must be that the penalty of not finishing on time is related to the delay in getting the expected benefits."

Everybody nods.

"Brian, let's go back to your specific case. Why is your company investing, how much did you say, six million, to expand the plant? What benefits do they expect?"

"We need the capacity." Responding to my signal to proceed, Brian adds, "We have a very nice product line, of which we cannot supply enough to the market. I see now. The damage to the company will be the delay in getting the additional sales."

"We want to quantify it," I remind him. "Now, a minute ago you were not sure if we need to know 'expected sales.' Do we need it?"

"Without a doubt."

I smile. "I told you that you know the answer. Just think clearly, that's all."

They laugh.

"Now that we've agreed that we need to know expected sales, can you tell it to us? How much more will your company sell due to the additional capacity?"

"The forecast is two million per month. A very conservative forecast. The consensus is that once we are up and running we will surpass it."

"Fine," I say. "Can we now answer 'what is the penalty of a delay?' Or do we need more data?"

"What are the margins on this product line?" Fred asks.

Before Brian can answer, I step in. "Fred, why do you want to know?"

"Because otherwise how can I calculate the impact on the bottom line?"

Remembering what I've learned from Johnny, I interject, "Margins are a lousy way of determining it, but for establishing order of magnitude it will suffice," and I gesture to Brian to answer Fred's question.

"It's a very good product," Brian explains. "The net margins are over thirty-five percent."

Now that there are more facts on the table, I repeat my question. "What is the penalty for the company of a one-month delay in completing the expansion project? Brian?"

He doesn't answer.

"Two million dollars sales per month times thirty-five percent net margin . . ." I feed it to him with a spoon.

"Seven hundred thousand dollars a month. I know how to multiply. But I don't buy it. This money will not be lost, it will just be postponed. Ah, I need to know the interest rate."

"Forget the interest!" Fred tries to help. "Did you ever hear about cash flow?"

"Cash flow is very important," I agree. "But in this case, also net profit is lost. Brian, why do you claim that money is not lost, only postponed? Because you assume that sales will be there also in the future. What other piece of data do we need in order to examine your assumption?"

"I don't know." Nor does anybody else.

I try to help. "Brian, how long do you think your company will be able to command such hefty margins on this product line?"

"Nobody knows. Maybe two years, maybe three. I see your point. It's not just money delayed, a major portion of it is money gone forever." He swallows hard. "We are talking about hundreds of thousands per month. That's huge."

Now I can return to my original question. "Do you think that the project team has a clear idea of the damage the company will suffer if the project is not finished on time?"

"No, they don't," he confidently answers.

"Not realizing the dollar impact of a one-month delay surely has an impact on the way your project team deals with your subcontractors?"

While he thinks about it I turn to the class. "It is surprising, but unfortunately this is the case everywhere. Most people involved in a project don't explicitly recognize the penalties associated with each month that the project is delayed."

"Before we start to discuss how we should negotiate with our vendors, I want every one of you to realize the magnitude of this phenomenon.

So, take your time and think about the projects you are involved in. Now that you know more, try to figure out the actual damage associated with a delay."

"We don't have to think about it," Mark responds immediately. "In our case the penalty is mammoth."

And he explains to the class his company's situation: a high-tech company captured in a frantic race, forced to release a new generation of products every six months or so. A few months' delay in their case means a substantial drop in market share.

I interrupt to highlight an important point. "In Mark's case the damage is much more severe than in Brian's case. Mark's company is not going to lose just additional sales, they are also going to lose existing market share."

"It's even worse than that," Mark continues. Since our stock value is based on expectations, a drop in market share means mammoth damage to our shareholders. And therefore to our job security."

"Is everybody involved in developing new products as aware of this as you are?" I ask, surprised.

"I don't think so," Ruth answers. "Few see the full ramifications."

I think Mark disagrees with her when he says, "Every project manager knows that it's important not to be late." But then he continues, "They know it because the pressure to finish on time is immense. But, as a project leader, I can tell you, they don't really know why. Until our executive vice-president explained it to the three of us, we didn't know. Maybe Fred did, but I didn't."

"Me, neither. I was not aware of the impact on the shareholders and the impact on the future of the company," Fred confirms.

"This is generally the situation," I conclude for the class. "Most people involved in the project, often including the project leaders, are not fully aware of the magnitude of damage associated with a delay. No wonder that when we negotiate with vendors or subcontractors we do not pay enough attention to their lead time."

"You may be right," Roger comments, "but it's too late. We have already conditioned the vendors to compete on price."

At first I'm surprised that Roger is bothering to participate. Then I realize that, at last, we are dealing with his subject.

I think I understand what he meant, nevertheless I check. "What do you mean by 'conditioned to compete on price'?"

He doesn't bother to explain. He just states, "Competing on lead time! It's beyond them."

Noticing my skepticism, he continues, "I don't believe that it is possible to explain to them that lead time is very important for us. Sometimes more important than price."

"What will happen," I suggest, "if in your request for proposals you write a sentence like 'above X price don't submit, above Y lead time don't submit a proposal.' Don't you think that will drive the message home?"

"To put a price in my request for a proposal?" He is astonished.

"Not a price. A cap on the price."

He doesn't answer. He thinks. So he is not as thick as I thought.

An attack comes from a direction I least expected. "Still, many vendors are conditioned to compete only on price," Ruth declares.

"Why do you say that?" It's my turn to be astonished.

"You know how many times I've tried to squeeze shorter lead times from a printing house? Every time we run into an emergency with our promotional material. Which means, very frequently. I try to offer more money, I beg, I plead. It doesn't help. They behave as if their lead times are cast in iron."

I struggle with it. It's hard for me to believe that's the case. But Ruth is very reliable. I ask some more questions. Ruth fully cooperates. She will not twist around the facts, but she struggles with me. Others contribute. Ruth is not the only one who has to deal with printers. Finally the picture emerges.

You go to a printer and ask for a quote for a brochure. They tell you four weeks. You come with all the needed final material in your hands, and you are willing to pay more, and they agree to do it in four days. They simply have had very bad experiences with clients wasting so much time making up their minds on all the details.

"So there is a way to trade lead time for money," I conclude. "The key is to understand the true impact for us, otherwise we will not be willing to pay for shorter lead times."

"We also have to understand the vendors' concerns," Ruth reminds me. "Otherwise, even if we are willing to pay, they will not be willing to commit."

I fully agree. Now that this issue is cleared up, I can raise the other problem. "We heard from Mark how important it is not to tell a completion date to the person doing the work."

"You do it," Mark emphasizes, "and you almost force the 'student syndrome'; then lead times cannot be shortened."

"But what do we do with vendors?" I continue. "We force them to commit to a delivery date. Exactly the opposite of what we should do."

"You're telling us not to ask for commitment to a delivery date?" Roger is back in the ring."

"That's exactly what I said."

"How are you going to convince a vendor to leave so much up in the air?" he sarcastically asks.

I don't have an answer. "By talking his language," I say.

He narrows his eyes. "Last time you agreed to come with me to a meeting with a vendor. Is your offer still open?" Smirking, he looks around.

I nod. Any other answer and I'll lose all credibility. Next time I'll be more careful ducking questions.

"Wednesday morning okay?"

"Yes," I quack.

"It will be interesting to see you talk the language of my vendor." Roger doesn't miss the opportunity to turn the dagger. They all laugh.

I give them a pile of homework.

When they've all left, Charlene approaches me. Oh, no. She saw it all.

"It was very interesting," she says. "I learned a lot."

I give her a dirty look.

"After this class, I have to rethink the whole subject of net-present-value. Something is terribly wrong there."

I don't know what she is talking about. But at least somebody is satisfied with this class.

"Six weeks? Can't you do it faster?"

"Impossible."

He is in his early fifties. Big mustache, all gray. And he talks confidently. Clearly he knows his business. What he forgot about special coating is more than I ever knew. What am I talking about? I know diddly about it.

Roger might know much more, but he is playing the dummy. I cannot expect any help from his side. He's just sitting there grinning to himself.

It's unfair. To talk the vendor's language you have to know something about the vendor. And I know nothing.

I flip through the proposal again. Most of it is meaningless to me. Every second word is technical jargon. But I do know how to read numbers, and the numbers are telling me that something is fishy.

This proposal is for coating three different molds. Each one takes a different number of hours to do, nevertheless, they are each quoted to be delivered in six weeks. I suspect that the lead time is not based on anything more than a general rule of thumb 'This type of a job, quote six weeks' type of rule.

The reluctance of the salesman to discuss it strengthens my opinion. But how can I prove it? Moreover, how can I persuade him that this 'six weeks' is not holy? I don't say a word.

Salespeople don't like silence. "I could have told you, like some of our competitors might, that we could deliver in five weeks. But we have a reputation to protect. Roger can tell you how reliable we are."

"Reliable?" Roger almost chokes. "What about . . ." Then he reconsiders. "You're as reliable as the others."

"That's unfair," the salesman protests.

"Well, slightly more reliable." He can't stop himself from adding, "Which is not a big deal."

"When we say six weeks," the salesman is firm, "we deliver in six weeks. And always first-class quality. We don't compromise on quality, like others sometimes do." And he gives us a whole story about coatings that peel, not theirs, God forbid.

When he finishes, I'm ready to start. "Let's take the big mold. You are charging for seventy-four point two hours. Remarkable accuracy. By the way, you must be computerized."

"Sure," he says proudly. "We use only the very best and latest technology."

"Do you work one shift?" I ask.

"No. In two of our processes we have two shifts." And he gives a long explanation. Listening to him you get the impression they invented efficient coating.

I let him finish and then say, "Seventy-four hours, even if all the work is done sequentially, does not make up six weeks. Using two shifts, it's closer to one week."

"You have to add curing time and drying time. It all adds up."

"How long can it take? Curing and drying are twenty-four hours a day." And I make a wild, totally unfounded speculation, "So another two days. Where do you get the six weeks from?"

"Closer to four days. This is a three-layer job." Then realizing that he's still far from justifying six weeks, he adds, "And there are other jobs in the shop. We are a big place."

"Eleven people," Roger murmurs.

"So if you gave this job top priority," I charge on, "you could finish it in less than two weeks."

"We cannot give it top priority," he protests. "Every client wants his job rushed." His face reddens. "If we give everything top priority, our place will become a zoo. It's out of the question. I'll never allow it."

The way he talks one might think that he was the owner, not just a salesman. Then I realize, with eleven people in total, maybe he is the owner.

It's not wise to push a person into a corner, so for now I drop this topic. "Can we go over the cost calculation?" I suggest.

He relaxes. Here is a place he can tell me whatever he wants, and there is no way I can expose him.

Taking his time, he explains all the details. It's important to him to show me how cost efficient they are. I let him persuade me that he makes only six-percent profit on these jobs. Roger is yawning.

"There isn't much profit in this business," I say.

Roger wants to protest, but our coating man doesn't give him a chance. He immediately starts with another lengthy story that is supposed to demonstrate how careful they are with their quotes. One might get the impression that their mission in life is to save money for their customers. Maybe he is the salesman after all.

When the flood stops, I say, "You need more net profit. Roger's company needs shorter delivery times. I suggest you put it in your proposal."

"Put what?" He's confused.

"I'm not asking you to give anyone first priority," I clarify. "But, I think you should add some options. Options that trade price with lead time."

He still doesn't understand.

"Something like . . . doubling your profit for three-week delivery."

"Three weeks is out of the question!" He reacts immediately.

I don't know what else to say, when he continues, "But maybe we can do it in four weeks."

"It might work," I say. "So suppose they give you the molds in, let's say, March . . ." I look at Roger.

"There about," Roger confirms.

"Suppose they give them to you sometime in March . . ."

"I need the molds," the coating man says. "And I need clear drawings. From the minute everything is in my hands you can count four weeks and the molds, perfectly coated, will be delivered. But then I'm paid six percent more. That's the deal?"

"What date are we talking about?" Roger interferes.

"It doesn't matter," comes the grumpy answer. "I deliver four weeks after I get everything I need. All the pieces of the mold, not one missing, and all the drawings. Only then the clock starts."

He stresses it so much, it's apparent that here is where he usually loses the time. It's similar to what I learned from Ruth regarding printing houses. The same phenomenon.

"There is another thing," I say. "The smaller mold, is it possible, for that job only, that when it arrives, you drop everything else and work on it."

"No way," he says flatly.

I want to demonstrate to Roger that it is possible to build a resource-buffer even when dealing with a subcontractor, so I try again. "How much more money do you want for it?" If this mold were on the critical path, it would pay us to pay more.

"I told you, no way. I can't run my shop from one day to the next. That's not the way to run a place."

Remembering what Mark is doing in his project, I try the same. "I'm not talking about that. Ten days before you get all the pieces of that mold and all the drawings, you will be notified."

He thinks about it, and then declines. "A lot can happen in ten days."

"Suppose they give you notice ten days before they plan to ship it. Then, three days before. And then a day before. That way you could comfortably plan your work."

"I don't know," he says.

"What about another six percent for this service. It would triple your profit on this job. Why won't you add this option to your proposal? One of the major criteria to choose a winner is vendor responsiveness. Be more responsive, for a price of course."

"Fine, I'll add it." He turns to Roger. "When do you want the modified proposal?"

"Wait," I interrupt. "There is one more thing."

"What is it?" he manages not to snarl.

"You want to know, in advance, what is coming your way."

"Without it, forget it."

"Forget what?" Roger aggressively asks.

"If you don't give me the notices, as we discussed, forget it. I'm not going to give first priority to the small mold. No matter how much you want to pay."

Before Roger has the opportunity to mess it all up, I step in. "You are right," I pacify the coat-man. "To run your business properly, you must have a clear idea of what's coming your way. So does Roger."

"What do you mean?"

"When you deliver the coated molds," I explain, "that's not the end of the story. There is a lot of work that depends on them. Roger's company needs to get advance notice from you when to expect each mold back."

"Four weeks. I told you."

"A lot can happen in four weeks," I flatly repeat his phrase. "Besides, on the small mold, we do expect to get it in less than four weeks."

"I see." He thinks it over. "Once a week. That's all I can do. I'm not going to turn my place into a paper nightmare. Once a week is all I can do." He turns back to Roger. "When do you want the modified proposal?"

"I don't want it," Roger flatly says. "Why waste my time. Let's finalize this deal now."

Less than ten minutes later, a happy salesman walks out.

"If I hadn't seen it with my own eyes, I wouldn't believe it," Roger says. "A vendor who doesn't insist on dates? What a dummy."

A teacher is supposed to like his students. But with some

students it's mission impossible. "Why call him a dummy?" I'm impatient with him. "Do you think that he should care, now, in January, if the work will be at the beginning of March or at the end?" Then I add, "At this stage, negotiation is on lead time. Not on date. That's always the case. Your problem is that once you agree on lead time, in those rare cases you bother to argue about it, then you yourself force the date. It's not the vendor, it's you."

I cannot stop myself from adding, "And as you noticed, if you talk the vendor's language, there is no problem. The vendor is willing to commit to much shorter lead times, for money."

"One swallow doesn't yet mean it's spring," he plays it down. Then he grins. "But I must admit, just for you I picked the most conservative vendor I know."

I control my desire to punch him and instead remark, "He can't be so conservative if they use the latest technology."

"They don't. But they have some real experts, some real meisters."

I want to leave, but I have a problem. I know Roger just wanted to humiliate me, to show that I'm full of hot air. I won, but Roger will never admit it to the class. That's why we agreed that if I succeeded in moving the vendor to modify his proposal, I would get copies of the original and modified proposals. That way I could show the class a real case demonstrating that a vendor can be persuaded to trade lead time for money, and that a vendor does not insist on exact starting times, and definitely not on a delivery date.

But now there will be no modified proposal.

"Tell me, Roger, how come you actually agreed to pay more? Where are you going to get the additional budget?"

He shrugs. "I've been in this business for a long time. I have my cushions."

"And top management? Will they agree?" I try to punch a hole in his greasy self-assurance. "I suspect that paying for shorter lead times is against some cost-saving policies."

It doesn't work. "I took care of it."

"May I ask how?"

"First, I had a meeting with my boss, the VP of finance. Then he dragged me with him to tell it to the president. I explained the bottom line impact of shortening our project lead time. That trivial stuff you talked about. They took to it like fish to water. No problem."

I can't believe my ears. Such a thing coming from Roger? It's hard for me to grasp. I considered Roger my most nasty, bitchy, cynical student, and the last one I expected to take initiative. Nasty and bitchy he is, but he sure can move.

"By the way," I hear him say, "next week I have important meetings with three more vendors. Is it possible for you to join in? Soften them up a little for me, you know?"

I'm wondering how to answer, when he continues.

"Of course, I can't ask you to do it for free. Will five hundred dollars a meeting do?"

"Only if you prepare a presentation for the class on how to negotiate shorter lead times with vendors."

At last I reached him. He makes faces, but I'm firm.

In the car, it dawns on me. That's fifteen hundred dollars. Judith will love another weekend in the Big Apple.

Chapter 19

Mark, Ruth and Fred update Isaac Levy. He wants to go over the details. It doesn't take long; the project is not far from completion. The project buffer is still nine weeks. The remaining feeding buffers also look healthy.

"Looking good," Isaac says when they finish. "Almost too good to be true. I must say that at the beginning I was quite skeptical, but you can't argue with the results."

"We are going to deliver two months ahead of time and without compromising on any of the original specs," Mark is confident.

Levy smiles.

"As far as I'm concerned, it's a world record," Mark concludes.

Still smiling, Isaac asks, "What is the chance of a piece of bread falling with the butter-side down?"

"Fifty percent," Fred answers.

"In this place it's closer to one hundred," Mark corrects him.

"You are too optimistic," Isaac says. "The chance of a piece of

bread falling with the butter facing down . . . is directly pro-
portional to the price of the carpet."

They are all in a good mood, so it takes some time before they
stop laughing.

"You haven't finished yet," Levy reminds them. "The final
tests on the modem just started. Anything can still happen."

"So I shouldn't have started the wheels rolling in marketing?" Ruth is not sure anymore.

Levy thinks about it.

"We can't afford to surprise them," Ruth tries to persuade
him. "If we do, all the gain we make here will be wasted there."

"You are right," Levy says.

"So what do you think?" Mark pushes Levy. "Suppose that
the final tests do not reveal anything catastrophic, do you think
we made it?"

Isaac looks at the three of them. They are quiet, waiting for
his verdict. "Let's straighten things up," he says. "Even if the
final tests reveal some bad news, it has nothing to do with what
you three have done. We were looking for a way to significantly
shrink the development time and you pointed out such a way.
But . . ."

He pauses for a few seconds to organize his thoughts. The
three do not dare to even blink.

"But, there is still a lot to do until the way is clear. Right now
I have more questions than you have answers. We are only at
the beginning."

He tries to give them an example of what he means. "When
you started to implement this radical method, the A226 was in
the final stages. Not that I'm trying to put down what you did,
you have done a wonderful job. But I would like to see how
your method works on a full project. From start to finish."

"I don't see much difference," Marks argues.

"You may be right, but until we try it, we don't know. Besides," Isaac adds, "don't you think it would be interesting to
find out by how much your method can shorten the development time?"

They do not answer.

"There is another thing that troubles me," he says. "I see how you made it work with one project, but I don't clearly see how it will work with many. Our projects interact with each other, you know."

"I know," Mark murmurs. Then, gathering his courage, he looks into Isaac's eyes and says, "There will always be some loose ends."

When Isaac doesn't answer, Ruth adds, "When are we going back to our regular jobs?"

Isaac turns to Fred, "Do you have a question as well?"

"Yes," he says. "We were promised that if we succeeded we would get ten thousand shares each. What are the criteria for our success?"

"Ten thousand shares each is a lot of money," Isaac answers. "Do you think that you earned it?"

They don't answer. He continues. "Are you willing to gamble that your method works? Always? In how many cases have we checked it? From start to finish, not even once. If you were developing a modem, would you accept it as a final product? At the stage that we are now it's only a promising prototype. Don't ask me what the criteria are. You know. You know when something can be declared good enough."

"I think we would like to have a more tangible target," Ruth says quietly. "I know I would."

"I cannot commit to any numbers, but I can tell you that when it's clear that your method is going to become the norm in our company, you have definitely delivered. Is that good enough for you?"

"It's good enough," Mark says firmly. He looks at the others. They nod.

"You said there are no budget limitations," Fred reminds Isaac. "Can we hire the help of our professor? I don't think it's fair to continue to use Professor Silver's kindness, and we need more of his time."

"Sure, good idea. Offer him the standard consulting fee, a

thousand dollars per day. Does three days a month sound about right?"

"Will do," Mark answers for the three of them.

"Anything else you need, think tank? Fine. Keep up the good job and continue to keep me posted."

Mark's phone call has me feeling giddy. Laughing, I head downtown. I'll find Judith a real Valentine's Day present in the jewelry store. Tonight, for once, my wife will get a gift she deserves. Finally.

Well, easier said than done. I don't know much about jewelry, and the saleswoman in the store isn't much help, although she tries. She even models the jewelry for me. But Judith has thick golden hair, high cheekbones and a beautiful long neck, and this lady . . .

I think I've seen every piece of jewelry in the store at least four times. Finally, still hesitant, I make my decision. Just to be on the safe side, I also go and buy a box of the fanciest chocolates I can find.

After Judith and I finish dinner, we go into the living room. That's when I give her present to her. Not the chocolate, the earrings.

She doesn't have to tell me how much she likes them. Her blue eyes tell it all. They glitter now, like the aquamarines that dangle from her ears. She truly loves them.

When we sit down, I start to tell her about the consulting job with Genemodem.

"Another three thousand dollars a month," Judith jumps to her feet. "Darling, that's a fortune."

My ears prevent my smile from becoming even broader.

"I told you that you'll manage." Judith starts to dance around. "I told you that if the university doesn't have the sense to appreciate you, others will."

I sink deeper into the couch. "Yes, you did," I admit.

"How much do you make now from consulting? More than from teaching?" She closes her eyes and starts to slowly turn around and around with her arms spread out. "And next year, when more companies find out about my brilliant husband, we'll have nothing to worry about."

I wish she were right.

She takes one look at me and stops spinning. "Darling, I'm sorry. I know how much you love teaching, but only last month you told me that consulting is a form of teaching. Isn't it?"

"Depends on how one does it."

"The way you do?"

"I think I can be happy with this type of work, but . . ."

She sits down next to me. "What's the problem, darling?"

"Next year I'll be out of the university," I start to explain. "I won't have corporate managers as students. And on my own, I'll never succeed in getting any consulting contracts. Please Judith, let's not fool ourselves, I don't have what it takes to sell myself. I can try, but, let's face it, what's happening now is not the beginning of a successful consulting business."

She takes both my hands. "We'll see. I have more faith in you than you have." Then she adds, "In the meantime we are rich."

"I wouldn't say that," I laugh. "But, I agree, an additional three thousand dollars a month can make a huge difference in our life. It will make a real dent in our pile of debts."

"And that will make a huge difference in our life?" Judith asks softly.

It takes me awhile to realize how insightful her question is. She is right. It won't really make any difference. I know I will find something for next year. Nothing spectacular, but I'll make a living. Reducing our debts would be nice, but it won't make a huge difference. Certainly not huge; maybe not even significant.

"What are you suggesting we do?" I ask.

"How long will your work with Genemodem last?"

"Four months, maybe six. By then they won't need me anymore," I answer, giving her my best evaluation.

She takes her time, choosing her words carefully. "Rick, for the last thirteen years we have had to count every penny."

"We should have," I tease her.

"Maybe, for the rest of our lives we'll have to do the same."

"I'm afraid so," I say bitterly. "There is no point in dreaming about an academic chair. Not anymore."

"It's okay, darling." She looks deeply into my eyes. "I mean it." After a pause, she continues, "Rick, can't we, for once in our lives, feel that we have enough? For six months? Even for four months."

I try to digest what she is saying. She wants us to spend it all. It's crazy. It's crazy, but it makes sense.

"Think about it as an investment," she says. "We will invest the money in what is most valuable. Good memories. Good, lasting memories."

I think about it. Judith doesn't press me. She just sits there, staring at the fireplace. The more I think about it, the more sense it makes.

Finally, I agree. "As the money comes, it will go."

She smiles at me. Proudly. And I know I have made the right decision.

"We are going to have the best winter and spring of our lives," I promise her. "Easter in the Bahamas. No, a cruise." She starts laughing. "Better still," I say, "I'll leave it up to you. You do the planning."

Miriam is not at her desk. I poke my head into Jim's office. "Jim, I'm stuck and I need your help."

"What is it?"

I interpret that as an invitation and walk in, closing the door behind me.

He puts his pen down and leans back in his chair. "There is one bad thing about teaching. You have to go over the homework assignments you give them."

"Give it to your Ph.D. students. Why lean on them less than you used to lean on me?"

"I wish I could," he sighs. "But you see, because of Johnny's ideas, I changed so much of my systems course that my Ph.D. students are as new to this material as the undergrads. But, enough crying on your shoulders. What do you want?"

"To cry on your shoulders," I smile. And then, more seriously, "I have a problem. I don't know what to do in a case where several projects are done by the same pool of people and one of the skills is a bottleneck."

"Rick, since when are you interested in such theoretical cases?"

"That's the problem," I sigh. "It isn't theoretical. That's what I'm actually facing in Genemodem. Several projects, and digital processing, which is involved in all of them, is a bottleneck."

"So, why don't you go about it systematically? First step: 'Identify the constraint.' Is there a problem finding the bottleneck in your case?"

"Suppose not. But why do you decide that the bottleneck is the constraint?"

Jim uses the words 'constraint' and 'bottleneck' synonymously. No wonder his response is, "I don't get you."

"We are talking about projects. In a project the constraint is the critical path."

"Hmm. The bottleneck is a constraint for sure, but you're right, so is the critical path. What are we supposed to do in the case of two constraints?"

"More than two," I say. "Each one of the projects has its own critical path."

I can almost hear the wheels turning in Jim's head. Many constraints . . . Can we deal with each project in isolation? No. Because if we do that, we'll be forced to ignore the bottleneck, and that's wrong. "Rick, I don't know. I don't know even where to start thinking about such a problem."

"Me, neither, and I haven't been thinking about it for five minutes, but for five days."

"Johnny might help." Jim picks up the phone.

A few minutes later Johnny enters. Half of his shirt is out and his hair is a mess, clear signs that we interrupted him in one of his brainstormings. I feel guilty.

He heads directly to the couch. "Thank you for saving me from my misery. I woke up with some stupid problem, and since then I've been chasing it in circles. Tell me that you have a simple, elegant problem for me, something I can solve in five minutes and feel good about."

"We have," Jim promises him.

I start to explain.

Johnny listens and then says, "I don't know enough about projects."

"And we don't know much about constraints. So can you help me?"

"The blind leading the blind," he sighs. "Fine, let's put our heads together. But first, Jim, I need coffee."

"Miriam!"

Chapter 20

I'm in my office going over homework assignments. I teach four courses, and I'm a firm believer in homework. Unlike Jim, I like reading it. It's time consuming, but it's the only way to get real feedback; what I taught well, where was I too quick, what I mistakenly took for granted. So I'm not bored. Besides, some of the mistakes the students make are hilarious.

A knock on the door.

"Yes?"

Ted sticks his red head in. "Can I interrupt for a moment?" he asks politely.

"Sure thing. Have a seat." It's not time for student hours, but if it's important enough for him to come during the week, I have the time.

"I don't know how to do my homework assignment," he sighs.

"Since when are students concerned about such things?"

He laughs nervously. "This time it's important. You see, I know that we should shorten our lead time. And now, after what you taught us and what the Genemodem team have done, I'm beginning to think that maybe it's possible. But . . .''

"But what?" I encourage him to continue.

"Look. The homework assignment was to calculate the damage to our company, the damage resulting from delaying the completion of a project."

"Correct. So, Ted, what's the problem?"

"I can't find any damages, I can only find advantages. But that can't be true."

Desperately, he adds. "I wanted to implement it in our company. I even spoke with my boss, and he is open. But now I don't know any more. If shortening project lead times doesn't benefit my company, why should we bother doing it?"

"Hold your horses. Don't jump to hasty conclusions."

"That's why I'm here," he says flatly.

"Good. Let's take it slowly. Have you tried to follow Brian and Mark's examples?"

He shakes his head. "They are not relevant for me."

"Why?"

"They own their projects," he answers. "We are just subcontractors. In our case the owner of the project is the developer, not us.

I see what he means. The owner of the project is the one who reaps the benefits from the completed project. No wonder the damage of not completing the project on time effects mainly the owner. But there must be repercussions on everybody involved.

"Let me understand it a little better," I say. "For your company, what is the penalty of finishing a construction site three months late? Yes, I know, you are never that late. So let's say that due to changes requested by your client you finish three months later than the original date. Does that happen?"

"All the time. Forget what I said in class. Between these four walls, I don't remember one project that we finished on time, in spite of all the safety we put in. Everything that we covered in class, all the problems, we have them. But when you ask the real question, 'why should we care?' the answer is that we shouldn't.

There is no penalty for our company being late. On the contrary, it helps us."

"How come?"

Aggressively, he answers. "Let me tell you the full story. At the time we sign the contract, our prices are very low. Competition is so fierce that we don't have any choice. You can win or lose a bid on a three percent difference in price. Everybody is cutting everybody else's throat. Where do we make our money?" He pauses for a second as if waiting for me to answer.

I don't know the answer.

"On the changes!" And then he elaborates. "Our motto is, the client is always right. They want changes, we won't argue, we'll gladly do them, the more the better. But at this stage we are not afraid that our dear client will turn to our competitor, so they pay. Handsomely." Ted looks as if he has just revealed the secret of his trade.

Judith just finished major repairs on our house, so I know how much they charge for things that are not spelled out in the contract. I suspect that if Judith hadn't initiated changes, the contractors would have their ways of inducing her to ask for them. Come to think of it, they probably did. Who needs eight inches of insulation in the roof?

Ted is right. For his company, what's the point of finishing ahead of time?

Getting paid earlier? Can't be a major consideration, they get progress payments.

Before I give up, I try to understand more about his business environment. "Aside from the money you overcharge for the changes, what is the damage to your client of having the buildings ready three months late?"

"I don't know, but isn't that his problem?"

"Maybe. But let's think about it. Three months' delay. What might be the damage for him?"

"For the developer?" Ted thinks a little. "He will sell the apartments three months later than he expected."

I keep asking, "Is that a big deal for the developer? It must impact his cash flow."

"That might be a problem," he agrees. Then, slowly, he adds, "It might be a big problem."

"Why?"

"Most developers don't have enough capital; the investments are far too big. They borrow money. I don't think I know any developer who is not mortgaged to the hilt. Cash flow is their major concern.

"Actually, I can give you more than one example where a three-month delay bankrupted a developer." Smiling, he adds, "Thank God it's not our problem. We get paid one way or another . . . I think."

After a moment of silence, he says, "You might have a point. I'd better check how much money we lost because developers went bankrupt. As a matter of fact, their tight cash flow affects us all the time. They delay their payments to us. Which is a problem."

He stands up. "Thank you." He shakes my hand, and with a warm smile, he is gone.

"See you next weekend," I say to the closed door, and return to my work.

Not for long. Another knock on my door. I didn't know they turned my office into a train station.

"Come in."

This time it's Johnny. I stand up to welcome him.

"I haven't made any progress on bottlenecks in projects," I warn him.

"Neither did I," he smiles. "I came for something else. Charlene told me about something interesting she picked up in your class."

"If you mean 'net-present-value,' I don't teach it, and in spite of all Charlene's efforts, I don't even understand it. I know she claims the opposite, but . . ." And I leave the sentence open.

"I'm sure you teach many interesting things, but the one I'm particularly interested in is how to negotiate with vendors. The shorter lead time aspect."

I like this subject. I started to really like it after Roger gave his brilliant presentation. He described all four meetings, using such sharp and dry humor I almost started to like him.

"What do you want to know about it?"

"Everything." And then he explains. "You know that I'm connected to UniCo. You also know that UniCo is putting a large operation here."

Of course I know, who doesn't? "But isn't it well on its way?"

"Yes, it is. So much on its way that they started to get nervous that they are going to be late. I got a call to look into it; something has to be done to speed up the contractors. So here I am ready to learn anything you care to teach me about it."

It doesn't take as long as I expect. Johnny absorbs in less than half an hour what took me almost two sessions in class. This guy is like a sponge. When we finish, I summarize, "Remember, you have to offer money for lead time. On their own, construction companies will never do it. Shrinking lead times is against their interest."

That surprises him.

I tell him what I learned today from Ted.

Johnny listens. Intently. But then he says, "I don't buy it."

"Why?"

"I don't know."

That's not an answer.

When Johnny notices my expression he hurries to add, "There must be something wrong here, even though I can't put my finger on it."

And I thought that Johnny was all facts and logic. Now I start to suspect that he is as superstitious as the rest of us. "What possibly can be wrong?" I express my disappointment.

"You describe a situation where a win for the subcontractor is definitely a loss for the developer. According to the Theory of Constraints that is an impossibility. Win-lose situations do not exist."

What an argument. "So here goes your theory," I flatly say.

"No, Rick, every time it seems like a win-lose exists, it's only because we are looking at the problem too narrowly."

I don't respond. I'm not going to argue about ideology and I don't want to offend Johnny.

He leans his elbows on my table and covers his face. I keep quiet. It's embarrassing. What is he doing? Constructing cloud diagrams in his head? Exposing assumptions?

After what seems a long time, probably three minutes or so, he raises his head, and smiling, he says, "Here it is."

"What?"

"You talked about the impact delays have on the developer's cash flow. Rick, can we safely assume that finishing before time also impacts his cash flow?"

"Naturally."

"And usually cash flow is very important to a developer?"

"Yes."

"You also told me that Ted's market is very price sensitive. A three-percent price difference will decide which contractor wins the bid."

"Yup."

"How do you reconcile these contradictory facts?"

I'm puzzled. "I don't understand. What contradicts what?"

"If a month's difference in delivery is so important to the developer," Johnny starts to explain, "then promised lead time should be a major consideration in choosing a contractor. But you said that's not the case, that price is the overwhelmingly decisive factor."

"Yes, it is," I say, still not fully grasping where he's leading.

Johnny tries to explain it in a different way. "Rick, do you agree that shorter lead time is important to a developer?"

"No doubt."

"So the developer should press the contractor to shorten the lead time."

"How can they?"

"One way to 'encourage' a contractor to reduce lead time is to attach big bonuses to early completion and big penalties to delays."

He raises his hand to prevent me from commenting. He wants to better explain this point. "Let's not forget," Johnny continues, "that most of the developer's investment is tied up toward the end of the project, so a three-month early finish can easily double the developer's return on investment. Why shouldn't he offer the contractor a big bonus for that?

"On the other hand, if a delay can put a developer into bankruptcy, he should try to put an enormous penalty into the contract with the contractor. As far as you know, are such big bonuses offered and huge penalties demanded?"

There are some bids that have small bonuses, but nothing like what Johnny is talking about. But the bonuses are not the problem; penalties are. "Show me a contractor," I say, "who would agree to penalties, even small ones. Their margins can't support it. What do you want? That they'll go bust?"

"Not at all. But Rick, imagine a contractor who knows he can deliver three months faster than anybody else."

"There isn't one."

"If they will bother to implement what you are teaching, there will be," he presses.

"If you insist. But I don't see the point."

"Don't you see that such a contractor won't have to compete on price?"

"I don't get it." I'm not stubborn. I really don't get it.

"Look, contractors know about future projects well ahead of time. They have their connections, and updated lists periodically appear in their professional magazines. What a fast contractor has to do is get in touch with a developer before a formal request for proposal is out. Contractors usually have good connections with several developers, so it shouldn't be a big problem. And then, all our fast contractor has to do is persuade the developer to put, in the request for proposal, a demand for relatively short lead times and hefty penalties."

"Hefty bonuses, you mean."

"No. Penalties."

To persuade the developer to put in hefty penalties? It doesn't make any sense. Then it dawns on me. It makes perfect sense.

"I see your point. If the request for proposal specifies relatively short lead times coupled with penalties, no other contractors will dare to bid. The developer will get a much higher return on his investment with much less risk, and the fast contractor will make much more profit." I smile at Johnny. "You are right after all. What contractors have now is not a win-lose, it's a lose-lose. The developers suffer from long and unreliable lead times, and the contractors suffer from a throat-cutting, price-sensitive market."

"And the contractor who realizes it can have a tremendous competitive edge," Johnny continues my thoughts. "Such a contractor could take the market while commanding good prices. The problem is that, like everybody else in projects, contractors think that they cannot do a thing to cut their lead times. The first ones to wake up will make a killing."

When Johnny leaves, I start my search for Ted's phone number.

Chapter 21

A pink note is on top of the pile in my mailbox. "Please call Mr. Brad Newbolt." And a telephone number. Who is Mr. Brad Newbolt? Probably a salesman of some kind trying to interest me in something. I put it aside. There are more pressing things to do. Jim is all over me to complete our third article in the series. Not that it matters now, but I don't like to let Jim down.

I'm deeply into it when the telephone rings.

"Professor Richard Silver?"

When I respond, the voice says, "I have Mr. Newbolt for you."

"Wait," I say. What gives salespeople the guts to think that they are allowed to command other people's time? Interrupting whenever they want. "Who is Mr. Newbolt?" I demand to know.

A deep baritone answers, "I'm the president of Q.E.C."

I gulp. Charlie works for them.

"I've wanted to call you for some time," he continues. "I'm very impressed with your work. We are using it, and it works very well."

"Thank you," I say. So Charlie also implemented it. He didn't say a word about it. Did he?

"Can I invite you to give us a lecture? I mean, to the YPO."

Y . . . P . . . O . . . ? I try to decipher the acronym.

I don't have to. "YPO is the Young President's Organization," he explains. "We get together every month for dinner, a small group. Only presidents of companies. Pullman from Genemodem is in our group. We usually have a guest speaker, and we share experiences. I discussed it with the others, and we would all like, very much, to hear your ideas on projects."

I'm flabbergasted. "I'd be delighted," I politely say. Pullman? From Genemodem?

"Next Wednesday all right? A dinner talk."

"Sure."

I try to keep my head from swelling. Next Wednesday. So soon. Probably their originally scheduled, respected guest speaker canceled on them at the last minute. I'm just the fill-in. Still . . .

"I'll fax you all the details. It was a pleasure speaking with you, Professor Silver. We'll see you next Wednesday."

Before I lose my courage, I write a memo to B.J. A short memo, just saying that I'm still trying to get students to the Executive MBA program. That I'm giving a dinner talk to the YPO. And I don't forget to mention that Pullman from Genemodem will be there.

It won't help. How can it? But I don't see how it can hurt, and I'm in a really cheerful mood.

The meeting is in a private room at the Sheraton. The first person I see as I enter is B.J. Good thing I don't have castanets attached to my knees.

It's not five minutes before she succeeds in maneuvering me into a corner. "You can't imagine how many strings I had to pull in order to be here. I almost had to promise that I'd join the YPO."

She talks as if I'm the one to be blamed. Blamed for what?

"I'm counting on you to give an excellent presentation," she keeps on pressing. "Be practical. Don't talk just theory."

"What else can I talk about?"

"Of course you have to talk about the unique know-how the Executive MBA students learn in our program. But be practical. Stress how much money this know-how saves for their companies."

"But I don't know how much."

"Then talk about how much it can save them."

I was nervous before I came here. I was even more nervous when I saw B.J. But only now do I understand what real nervousness means. Thank God she leaves me. Before anybody else has a chance to corner me, I grab a waiter. No, I don't want a drink. I want to know where the toilets are.

A minute after I start my presentation, I'm cool as a cucumber. My transparencies are good. Concise and to the point. They also look good. Who would believe that I only printed the latest version at noon? Anyone who's worked with today's software.

They almost don't interrupt me. Very few questions. But they nod in the right places. They let me feel that I'm making sense, that they are with me. When I finish, they clap. More than just politely. Or maybe I fool myself?

Only when I sit down do I realize I didn't do what B.J. wanted. It wasn't on my transparencies.

Newbolt goes to the front. He formally thanks me, and then, to my surprise, he adds, "This stuff does work. We experienced it. A project that was hopelessly late is now back on track. We are now starting to manage every major project this way."

"Same here." Pullman says.

"Did you test it at Genemodem?" B.J. asks. There is no trace of surprise in her voice.

"Yes, we did. We are launching our new line two months ahead of the competition."

"That must be worth millions to your company," B.J. softly remarks.

"It helps."

Dinner is served.

Before coffee, B.J. takes over the discussion. Somehow she succeeds in causing them to feel guilty that they don't provide enough support for the university. It goes well until she starts pressing them to send more managers to the Executive MBA program.

Then it starts to backfire. They react by mocking the value of the general knowledge taught in universities. They talk about the "first year shock" and about the fact that they have to spend so much money training their already "educated" managers about what really counts.

B.J. fights back. One president talks about the fact that they do support the Executive MBA program. They pay seventy-five percent of the inflated tuition the college charges. Another president asks why the tuition for an Executive MBA is three times the tuition for the regular program.

She ducks it. Instead she claims, and proves, that they don't support their managers enough. "The two weeks they take classes in the summer they have to use their vacation time. Why? Don't you think that it helps your company for them to learn? Or maybe you think that these people, these hard-working managers who sacrifice their weekends to learn, who have to do their homework at night after work, don't need a vacation?"

They say they would do more if what was taught was more in line with things like they heard tonight.

That's all B.J. needs to hear. Masterfully she maneuvers them to agree to seriously evaluate a special track for Executive MBAs tailored to their needs. She squeezes the appointment of a committee of three presidents, or their delegates.

When we leave, she takes my arm. "Accompany me to my car. Richard, I'm afraid I grossly underestimated you. You did create a valuable piece of know-how."

It's dark outside, so she can't see me blushing. "I couldn't have done it alone," I explain. "If it weren't for Professor Fisher's new knowledge and Professor Wilson . . ."

"So you are a team. Even better."

We reach her Seville STS. One of these days I, too, will have a Cadillac.

"What do you think. Is it possible to create a full, two-year program that will bring real value? Something of the caliber they heard from you tonight?"

"I think so," I answer. I'm not just telling her what she wants to hear. Based on what I hear from Jim, Johnny and particularly from Charlene, I really think so.

"Good," she slides into her car. "I'll update Christopher. I'm counting on you to update the head of the Executive MBA program."

She takes off. I stroll to my car. The sky is full of stars.

Chapter 22

It's Saturday morning and I'm stuck. What am I going to teach them today? Originally I'd planned to raise the topic of several projects done by common resources of which one is a bottleneck, the topic I call "projects'-bottleneck." No doubt it would lead to a lively discussion. Maybe I could have gotten a clue or two out of it. But now it's too dangerous. Jim will be sitting in my class.

He decided to expand his systems course to also cover projects, and he "needs to get an impression of the students' level of knowledge." What could I tell him? Don't come?

I'm going over the outline I prepared for the course during the summer. Except for the first few lessons, there isn't much in common with what I have actually taught. There are many topics I've skipped, but for a very good reason. They are what some would call academic—resource optimization, sequence optimization, investment optimization. I call them irrelevant. So what am I going to do?

Maybe Jim will be sick? Wouldn't help much. Before the end of the year there are still four, two-hour sessions that I have to teach.

I go over the outline again. Nothing.

What am I looking for? A topic that is relevant; that excludes all optimizations, that I know well. That excludes almost everything else, definitely projects'-bottleneck. Don't even think about it. And the topic must be one that we haven't yet covered in depth. What's left?

Maybe I'll go over the buffers again? The conceptual difference between a project-buffer, feeding-buffer and a resource-buffer. How many of my students understand that resource-buffers don't change the elapsed time of the project? Not many, if any.

Good subject, but how much time can we spend on it? Half an hour? Relying on my students' ability to flounder and the fact that I don't have any other ideas, I decide that it's good enough.

"Good morning, class."

"Good morning."

"Good morning, guests."

"Good morning," Charlene and Jim answer.

Ten seconds gone. Didn't help much. I'd better start.

"Now that almost all of you have actual experience," I start, "experience implementing what we have learned, I would like to go back and examine the concepts."

They like it.

Before I can continue, Ruth raises her hand. "I have a problem with the concepts."

What a statement. It doesn't sound good coming from Ruth. I force myself not to look at Jim.

Trying to sound nonchalant, I ask, "What's the problem?"

"Suppose that on one of the noncritical paths we are so late that we have already exhausted the entire feeding buffer, and we have started to penetrate into the project buffer. On the critical path itself we are okay."

"Might happen," I agree. "You might run into a serious problem in one of the feeding paths. But what is your conceptual problem?''

''In the situation Ruth just described, isn't it true that the critical path has changed?'' Fred answers. ''That now the critical path starts at the operation where we have the problem?''

I think about it. Before I reach any conclusion, Mark tries to clarify. ''We defined the critical path as the longest chain of dependent steps, longest in time.''

''Correct.''

''Ruth is talking about a situation where we are working on a step, call it step N, which is on a path we considered noncritical. Nevertheless, right now step N is delayed to the extent that it is causing the biggest penetration into the project-buffer. Doesn't this mean that right now, the longest chain of steps, longest in time, is starting at step N?''

''What are you saying?'' Ted jumps in. ''That midway through the project, we'll change the critical path? That's crazy.''

''Why?'' I ask. I know why. I also see why it is necessary. But I have to gain time to think it over.

Ted seems stuck. His intuition is excellent, his verbalization lags behind. Fred answers for him; it's apparent to me that the think tank really thought it over. ''We put feeding buffers only where a noncritical path merges into the critical path. Changing the critical path will necessitate changing the location of many feeding buffers.''

''And that,'' Ted concludes, ''will mess up the whole project. We can't do that.''

''Agreed,'' Ruth says calmly. ''But on the other hand, don't you see what will happen if we don't do it?''

''No!'' Ted responds too hastily. The thought of rearranging everything every time we face a serious delay on a noncritical path scares him. It scares me too.

''If we don't do it,'' Ruth continues, ''we're ignoring reality. Let's face it, whether or not we like it, right now the critical path does start at step N. And this path is not protected from disruptions in other paths by feeding buffers. It is also not protected by resource buffers. So the chance of recovery is reduced. On the contrary, there is a good chance that the delay will intensify. Don't you realize that we must rearrange the project?"

"We're doomed if we do, doomed if we don't," Ted concludes.

"That's our conceptual problem," Ruth says.

I control the wave of panic starting to build in me. Conceptual problem? Conceptual problem! What an understatement. It may ruin everything we have done!

Why haven't we seen it in reality? Four projects did finish much earlier than expected, so our method does work. Maybe it's because all these projects were already well along their way when we started. But in all cases we had feeding buffers that were exhausted; we had the situation Ruth described, so the problem cannot be as big as it seems. Where is the erroneous assumption the think tank is making?

I don't have a clue. I also don't have time. The class is waiting. Not just the class, Jim as well. I turn to the board and start to write the cloud. The objective is to finish the project on time. One necessary condition is what Ted said. We cannot afford to rearrange everything. Which means don't formally change the critical path. The other necessary condition is Ruth's point, we cannot afford to leave the true critical path exposed, which means we must formally change the critical path.

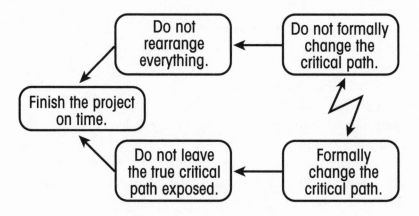

I use the trick Johnny taught me—concentrate on the arrow you dislike the most. Like Ted, I don't like rearranging the project midway; I don't want to formally change the critical path. It ruins the whole elegance of the solution, and will make it impractical. Moreover, we didn't have to do it in the projects we worked on. So what is the assumption there?

In order to not leave the true critical path exposed, we must formally change the critical path. Why? Because if we don't do it, the critical path will not be protected. Is it really the case? Now I see it.

Confidently, I ask the class, "What assumption do we make when we claim that if we don't formally change the critical path it will be exposed?"

They don't answer, so I ask again, "Are the original critical path and the true critical path very different from each other?"

"No," Ruth answers. "As a matter of fact, from the point where the two merge until the end of the project, they are the same. I see. So the only exposure is from step N up to, but not including, the step where they merge. In most cases there will be no additional feeding buffers involved, but what about the resource buffers we need for those intermediate steps?"

"That's not a problem," Mark says. "The original feeding buffer is exhausted. All my attention is on those steps anyhow."

"False alarm," Ruth apologizes.

"I don't think so," Charlie says. "I don't think this is a false alarm."

"Why?" asks Mark.

"Because, at least in my case, the critical path has started to jump all over. Every few days I have this problem. Frankly, I am about to give up."

"This is a very well-known phenomenon," Roger says. "Every project leader will tell you that the critical path changes during the project."

This is serious. I ignore Roger and concentrate on Charlie. He is not talking about a 'would be' problem or some generalization; he is talking about an existing problem. Charlie, especially after his president being so happy about what he has achieved, would not make such a statement unless the situation was really out of hand.

"Charlie, would you describe to us, in detail, what is actually happening?"

"It's frantic. Noncritical paths, where everything was fine, where the feeding buffers had not been touched, are starting to, all of a sudden, be a problem."

"A severe attack by Murphy," I try to be sympathetic.

"That's the weird thing," Charlie responds, "no special problems, no surprises, still, we are starting to fall behind."

Now I'm confused. And so is everybody else.

"Charlie, let's take it slowly. You are working on step N of a noncritical path, and . . . Now, tell us what happens."

"It's even weirder than that," he says. "I haven't started working on step N on the noncritical path, and this noncritical path becomes a real problem. Without doing a thing, I've exhausted the feeding buffer."

"What are you talking about," Ted speaks for all of us.

"Exactly what I said. I'm supposed to start on a certain step on a noncritical path, but the resource is not available."

"Where is the resource?" Ted asks impatiently.

"Working on another noncritical path."

"So move it."

"I can't. The noncritical path it's working on is also late."

"Miracle," Ted snorts. "Can't be. You're talking nonsense."

Charlie's face is red, but he controls himself, and doesn't answer Ted. He looks at me and asks, "Can I come to the board and show the situation?"

"By all means."

As he starts to draw, he says, "This is not my real project, but it will show you my problem." Two minutes later the diagram is drawn on the board.

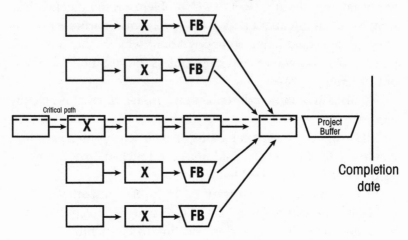

"What do the Xs stand for?" I ask him.

"They are steps done by the same specialist, of which we have only one. Assume that each step requires five days, and my feeding buffers are also five days. Do you see the problem?"

We look at the diagram. Charlie's problem is clear. It is also clear that this situation can happen in many projects. There are many contentions for X. For a period of time, X is overloaded and is falling behind. That's what is causing the delays, which are passed from one noncritical path to another. The feeding buffers are not enough to absorb these delays. No wonder his critical path is jumping from one path to another.

"It's obvious that I must acknowledge the limited capacity of X," Charlie says, "but then all our nice method collapses."

"Hold your horses," I say. "Let's go back to your diagram. What is the critical path here?"

"I don't know," he replies. "Not when I take the limited capacity of X into account."

I see the light. "Let's go back to our definition of critical path," I say confidently. "The longest chain of dependent steps, the longest in time. Don't ignore the limited capacity of X. Don't

ignore the fact that dependencies between two steps can be because they are performed by the same resource that has limited
capacity, so you cannot do both steps at the same time; you
must do them sequentially rather than in parallel. That is dependency."

"So what is the critical path?" Ruth asks.

"You tell me," I address the whole class. Jim is frantically
taking notes.

"We cannot start with X," Ruth says, "so we have to start
somewhere. Then immediately X becomes a problem and it does
determine the lead time. When we've finished with X we
haven't finished the project, there are still more steps to be
done."

"Exactly," I say. "Dependencies between steps can be a result
of a path or a result of a common resource. Why are we so
surprised that both dependencies are involved in determining
the longest chain of dependent steps?"

They seem to agree. "In general," I continue, "the longest
chain will be composed of sections that are path dependent and
sections that are resource dependent."

"So if we stick to the definition of a critical path, we get
something nobody calls a critical path?" Brian is puzzled.

"Why are you so surprised," Ted comments. "Nothing else
we do is common either."

"I agree. But we'd better straighten out the terminology. Let's
leave critical path to be what everyone else calls a critical path,
the longest path. But we know that what counts is the constraint, and the constraint is the longest chain of dependent
steps. Since we must acknowledge that dependency can be the
result of a resource, we better provide another name for the
chain of steps that are the constraint."

"Why not 'critical chain'?" Brian suggests.

Sounds good.

"Critical chain it is," I declare, before I'm flooded with other,
more bizarre, suggestions. People love to argue about names,

and I'm all of a sudden pressed for time. We have to hammer out all the ramifications of our new realization; it will not be restricted to just a change in terminology.

"Let's go back to Charlie's example," I say. "Again, what is the critical chain?" I love this new name. "Ruth?"

"I'm stuck," she says. "There are five steps that need the X resource. What sequence should I put them in? I don't know."

"Anybody have an idea?" I ask.

People love such riddles; suggestions come from all sides. As expected, many of them contradict each other. I fight my tendency to cut this useless discussion short. It becomes more and more convoluted, and the students get more and more confused. Good. After about fifteen minutes I decide they are ready.

"How much is eight times eight?" I ask.

Nobody answers. They probably wonder if I have lost it.

"Let me remind you that in projects we are not dealing with determinate numbers," I start to clarify the intent of my question. "When we say, for example, that a step will take eight days, do we really mean that it will take precisely eight days? Of course not. So how much is eight times eight?" And I write $(8 \pm 1) \times (8 \pm 1) = ?$

"The answer sixty-four is wrong. It gives a faulty impression of accuracy."

"Like an accountant who is forced to give an answer accurate to the cent, when even the first digit is questionable," Fred jokingly remarks.

"Correct." I like Fred's example. "Anyone see the relevancy to our debate?"

I help them. "It is a mistake to strive for accurate answers when the data is not accurate. Answers that pretend to be more accurate than the uncertainty embedded in the problem are not better answers."

Charlie does the connection. "Do you mean that the sequence in which we schedule X doesn't make any difference?"

"In some cases it does make a difference. There are endless

articles that deal with such cases. But the question is, does it make a real difference?"

Count on Ruth to ask, "What do you mean by 'real difference'?"

"A difference that is bigger than the uncertainty of the project," I answer. Before Ruth can question my answer, I do it. "What can we take as a reasonable yardstick for the uncertainty of the project?"

I let them think about it for a little while.

"The project buffer?" Brian hesitantly asks.

"Why?"

More sure of himself, he answers, "Because the project buffer is where we dampen the accumulated effects of all the uncertainties."

"What do you think?" I ask the class.

They think Brian is right. So do I.

"I don't know how many articles dealing with resource sequence optimization I have read," I tell them. "More than I care to remember. They contain many algorithms and heuristic rules to sequence resources. Between them, these articles consider everything you brought up here, and many more considerations that you haven't brought up. But I don't waste my time reading them anymore. Why? Because in each case the impact on the lead time of the project is less than even half the project-buffer."

Jim raises an eyebrow. Of course these articles don't specify a project-buffer. I use our rule of thumb to approximate it. Assuming the time estimation of each step contains safety, the project buffer is about one quarter of the lead time. I make a mental note to clarify it for him. But the students are not going to read these academic articles, so I charge on.

I bring the discussion back to focus. "Charlie is right in bringing up resource contention as something we must consider. There are projects where the contentions are too big for our feeding buffers to absorb. But there is a difference between considering resource contention and fiddling around with optimizing the schedule of these resources."

Charlie doesn't argue, he is too practical for that. "So what am I supposed to do?"

"Remove the contentions," Ted tells him.

"Easy to say."

Ted tries to explain that it is easy, but his explanation is so convoluted, even I don't understand it.

"Would you like to come up to the board and show what you mean on the example that Brian drew?" I suggest.

Ted is happy to do it, but he flounders a little. Everybody is trying to help, which doesn't help much. It's not what one might call an orderly session. But at last, Ted finishes. He made sure that no two steps done by X are scheduled in parallel.

"Can you highlight the critical chain?" I request.

He puts a dotted line.

"Since you changed the constraints, you must change the feeding buffers in accordance," I remind him.

With a little help from his friends he does it.

We examine the two diagrams, the one following the critical path that Charlie originally drew, and the one that Ted did. Quite a difference.

FB = Feeding Buffer

"It delays the completion date," Charlie is concerned.

"No, it didn't." Mark says. "It just prevented you from fooling yourself."

"Of course. What I mean," Charlie clarifies, "is that resource X delays the completion date. I think that I have to check what can be off-loaded to others."

"Or off-loaded not to other people but to other times," Brian comments.

Charlie gives him a glazed look.

Brian hurries to explain. "Resource X is not loaded for the entire time of the project. If you examine the details of his work you might find that some of his activities can be done much earlier or later. From my experience, I know that many times people batch activities together, not because they are needed to be done then, but to save time."

"You are right," Brian confirms. "A major part of this person's job is documenting her code. Some of the documentation is essential for the integration of the various parts of the software. This must be done immediately. But a lot of the documentation is needed only for future maintenance. Of course it's easier to complete the documentation while the code is fresh in your mind, but you are right, she can do it later."

I still look at the two diagrams on the board. I'm not bothered by the fact that the critical chain is longer than the critical path. That's to be expected. What overwhelms me is that almost all feeding buffers have changed their locations. Is this always the case, or are we misled by an artificial example?

I haven't seen it in the three projects that have successfully finished. But they were near completion; most activities were already done. No wonder there was little resource contention.

I raise the question to the class, asking them to relate it to their projects. How serious is resource contention?

Less than ten minutes later we have the answer: "It depends."

There are many projects where it does not matter; resource

contention is not a big deal. But for some other projects, and not just a few, it is.

"If there is resource contention," I remark, "the critical chain might be very different than the critical path. In those cases, what is the real danger in following the critical path rather than the critical chain?"

"It can lead to catastrophes." Charlie is alarmed. "That's what happened to me. The critical path is jumping all over. You lose control."

"It is even worse," Mark says in his deep voice. "Look at the two diagrams on the board. The feeding buffers, not to mention resource buffers, are in the wrong places; the constraint is not protected."

"And we know what happens then," Ted joins in. "Murphy is just waiting for it."

"We'd better check all our projects," Fred says to his friends. "I'm sure that we have resource contentions. A lot."

"Good," I say. "Exactly what are you going to do?"

Mark answers. "First we are going to add the resources to our PERT charts. They are not clearly marked in all projects. Then we are going to . . . " He stops.

"How are we going to ensure that steps done by limited re-sources will not be scheduled in parallel?" Ruth is concerned.

"That's my problem," Mark says, and then adds, "rather than drawing the steps on paper, we'll have to use something more flexible. For each step, we could cut a piece of paper so that the length represents the time. This way we can move them around until there is no contention."

"Good idea," Ruth agrees. "Maybe we can find suitable soft-ware."

I look at my watch. "Continue," I urge them.

"Once all contentions are removed, and I promise not to spend too much time playing with the sequence, then we iden-tify the critical chain. And then we put in the feeding buffers." Relieved, he adds, "This will change some dates, but it doesn't change the way we learned to manage a project."

"What happens if you find a few chains that take about the same time?" Brian asks.

Mark looks at me for the answer.

"Choose one, any one," I say. "And in order to prove that I'm right, here is your homework assignment. Take the project you are working on, and do what we said today."

"We'll do it anyhow," Brian comments.

"Right. But for me, add the answer to your question. If a few chains have approximately the same length, why doesn't it matter which one you pick, as long as you pick one."

As they are leaving, Jim approaches. "Your style of teaching is really something," he compliments me. "It's like new knowledge is created right in front of the students' eyes. Fascinating."

I don't have the courage to tell him how much he is right, that before this lesson I never suspected there was something like a critical chain.

Chapter 23

"As you know," Christopher Page says in his polished baritone, "we succeeded in persuading local companies, some of them very major, to form a committee. The committee's task was to reach a consensus on what these companies would like us to teach."

Apparently B.J. is not happy with the way Chris is putting it. "Our Executive MBA program is the most lucrative program we have. Unfortunately, we don't enroll enough students in it. This is the first time we're talking directly with organizations about our Executive MBA program," she emphasizes. "The presidents of the organizations who formed the committee told me that they don't send more students to Executive MBA programs because these programs are not tailored to their specific needs."

"In the last three weeks," Chris continues, "Jim spent many hours with the members of the committee, helping them verbalize their requirements. This paper is the results of their efforts." He hands a thin document to B.J.

Very thin. The first page is just a title: "Special Executive MBA Program."

The second page contains a relatively short list of topics. It doesn't take long to read.

"We will not have any problems conforming to their requirements," Chris says to B.J. "As a matter of fact, I think that even today we cover all of them. What do you think, Jim?"

"Yes," Jim says flatly. "If you ignore the somewhat strange verbalization, it's all the standard topics; projects, production, systems, finance, managing people, marketing. Nothing is special about it. It's the standard topics covered in every MBA program."

B.J. is slightly impatient. "This is an opportunity we cannot afford to miss. And in order to make it work, our program must be special. If we continue to do what we have done, which is what everybody else is doing, we will continue to get the same unsatisfactory results. My question is, how can we make our program special?"

"The key is on the next page," Jim says. "The problem is not with the subjects covered, but with the content and the method of delivery. Look at the next page."

"The knowledge taught does not bring value to the company," B.J. reads the first item.

"How can they say such a thing?" Chris is indignant.

"Easily," B.J. flatly responds. "The question is, can we do something about it?"

"I believe we can," Jim says. "Take, for example, Johnny's new production course. I heard from some of the students that they have already implemented this knowledge and gotten impressive results. In their departments they cut the inventory while improving volume. Or Charlene's course, in accounting, it's fantastic!"

"A fantastic course in accounting?" Chris cannot hold back his astonishment.

"Yes," Jim says. "What she teaches now about investment justification is of great value. I've personally heard stories from our students of how they used this knowledge to save hundreds of thousands of dollars for their companies."

"Hard to believe," Chris murmurs.

Jim pretends he doesn't hear. "Allow me also to say that my systems course, the way I have radically modified it this year, is also bringing value. But the best, no doubt, is Richard Silver's course. You have heard about it?"

"Of course," B.J. responds. "But may I ask what happened? You've all taught these courses for ages. How come now, all of a sudden, they are all so great?"

"It's Johnny Fisher," Jim responds. "He brought the break-through from UniCo, and we've all built on it. It had a major impact on what we teach. Almost everything had to be modi-fied. Chris, you heard his colloquium. . . ."

"Only the first fifteen minutes; there was an important meet-ing I had to attend. But I did hear very good things about it."

Can it be that the dream team I was praying for exists in my university? B.J. wonders incredulously. She reads the second item, "The examples used in class are too artificial."

"That's a real problem," Chris says. "For quite some time I have been pushing for more extensive use of the Harvard Busi-ness School case studies. But you know how tough it is to over-come inertia, especially among us professors."

"The Harvard cases are a step forward, but I'm afraid they are not good enough," Jim ventures.

"What do you mean?" Chris is surprised.

"The problem with cases is that they are deterministic," Jim explains. "Either the data is given or not. But reality is not like that. Reality contains many things that are malleable, vague, even debatable."

"True," B.J. agrees, "but there is nothing we can do about that."

"I think there is. Rick has shown us the way."

"Richard Silver?" B.J. checks.

"Yes. In his course, all the problems that they work on are real. They are problems that the students bring from their work. I agree that it's not so easy to use his style of teaching, but one thing is for sure, he is very successful with it."

"Fine. And the last item is, 'Students do not acquire problem-solving skills.' Well, obviously in Richard's class, they do."

"Correct," says Jim. "But that's not enough. Solving a few problems is not sufficient. We have to teach them how to do it systematically for every subject."

"That's a tall order," Chris comments.

"It is," Jim responds. "But with the thinking processes Johnny brought from UniCo, it's much simpler than one would think. We don't teach enough of it. But now that the rest of us have learned it, we are going to integrate it into all our courses. It will also help us use Rick's teaching method. Not everybody was born with his natural talent." After a second he adds, "It's not only possible, it's mandatory."

B.J. is trying to absorb all the good news, when Jim quietly continues, "There is one major problem, you know. How are we going to convince companies that our Executive MBA Program is of such value?"

"It won't be easy," B.J. agrees. She contemplates ways. None look promising. "Do you have any ideas?" she asks.

"The four of us were talking about it, and we did come up with an idea. But it's too unconventional."

"Carry on," she says softly.

"I think the major problem is that companies no longer believe that a person finishing an Executive MBA program has become a much better manager due to it. They don't see the tangible benefit to the company. So, why don't we promise it to them?"

"What do you mean?" Chris asks.

"Something like . . . For example, can we offer that the companies pay for the education only after the student has used his knowledge to bring the company benefits of at least one hundred thousand dollars? It's not such a big risk. You see, the mistakes companies make today are so fundamental the four of us are confident we can deliver such benefits, at least until our knowledge becomes standard practice in these companies. But by then the value of our teaching will be established."

"Out of the question," Chris exclaims. "We are a university. We are not some fly-by-night consulting firm. We don't have to prove ourselves."

"Yes, we do," B.J. says. "It's about time we got off our high horse. We do not deliver enough value; we hear it constantly. We do have to prove ourselves."

"No other university would think of offering such a thing. It's embarrassing."

"Listen to yourself," B.J. tells him softly. " 'No other university would think of such a thing.' You are right. They won't offer it because they can't deliver. Moreover, if no other university would think of offering such a deal, it is even better for us."

Chris shakes his head. "We don't offer deals. It's craziness."

"I think we'd better think it over," B.J. says calmly. "With open minds. Thank you, Jim. You opened my eyes, and in more than one way."

When Jim has left, Chris turns to her, "B.J., we are a university, not a bunch of gamblers. What's gotten into you?"

"Tell me, Chris. Do you believe what Jim told us, all these great things?"

"I've known him for over twenty years now. He is one of the most solid and reliable people I know. What he told us sounds hard to believe, but if he says they can deliver, they can."

"So it's not such a big gamble."

Chris starts to protest, but B.J. stops him. "Let's not argue; let's do our homework first. Before next week let's each talk with one president, not necessarily from the companies that formed that committee. Let's see what is needed to persuade these business people that we have an excellent program for them."

"I'm not going to offer any crazy deals," Chris is adamant.

"I didn't ask you to. Just try to persuade them that we have an excellent MBA program. Stress the points that we discussed: that the program will bring value to their companies, that it uses their real-life scenarios and that it will teach their managers to solve problems better. Let's learn what it takes to persuade them."

"That, I can do."

"Oh, yes, Chris, there is something else. It looks like this Richard Silver is a real gem."

"He is, and we are going to lose him, since you won't approve any tenure."

"We cannot afford to lose him. Submit the papers; I'll sign them.

"Don Pederson, please."

"May I ask who's calling?"

"Professor Fisher."

"Hello, Professor Fisher. Just a moment, please."

Music comes on, but not for long. "Johnny. How are you?"

"Fine, Don. Got a moment?"

"Always. What's up?"

"I think I've done my part of what we discussed last month. It's your turn to move."

"So soon? Are you sure?"

"I think so," Johnny says in a tone that indicates more confidence than the words imply.

"Tell me more." Don, true to his nature, wants to make his own evaluation.

"If I understood you correctly, you invested in the five of us so that you would not have to invest so much in every person you hire."

"Correct. There is no sense in UniCo having to educate every new employee, when that is supposed to be the job of the universities."

"Our university is ready," Johnny says, and then elaborates. "This year's graduates from the Executive MBA program are thoroughly indoctrinated in the throughput world. They feel comfortable with Theory of Constraints applications in production, finance, in systems, and listen to this, Don, in project management."

"So it's not just you teaching it." Don is pleased.

"Of course not, one person doesn't teach all these subjects. All the professors involved in the Executive MBA program are contaminated. And Don, they are doing an excellent job."

"How do you know? Are you judging by their grades?"

"You taught me too well for that, and besides, final exams are more than a month away. I'm using your criteria: results achieved by the students in their own companies."

"Great. What about marketing and the learning-organization aspects?"

"There is movement there as well. But that's not the issue. Don, I think we have crossed the biggest obstacle; the dean and the president of the university are all for it. They are launching a special MBA program that is centered around TOC. And listen to this. They are marketing it to local industry, based on results to be achieved in reality. Talk about an offer that can't be refused. Next year we are going to run three of these programs in parallel."

"That's good. But Johnny, what about the other aspect? You know it is as important, if not more so.

"You mean demonstrated, practical, research ability? I told you we developed the application for project management. It's already been tested in several companies. It gives the same type of astonishing results as the other applications of TOC."

"We need that," Don says. "We are not doing so well managing projects."

"Yes, I know," Johnny replies. "I've heard the facility you're putting up here in town has already slid six months behind schedule. But Don, this application is very powerful. It was tested on new-product development as well, and it's working."

"Fabulous. It looks like you've covered all the necessary ground work. It is time for my involvement."

"Definitely. If you want our university to teach this practical know-how to our undergraduates as well, you'd better move now. By the way, what progress have the other four professors made?"

"Not bad. It looks like we will have hubs in an engineering school and in human resources. But judging by what you say, you are the most advanced. Tell you what. In three weeks I'm coming to your neck of the woods to straighten up our operation there. Maybe it would be a good idea if you could arrange a one-day rush course for me in this project management?"

"No problem, but don't you think you have to meet with the dean of the business school?"

"Johnny, I know how to handle such things. What I have to do is to suggest that this knowledge will be taught at the undergraduate level as well. If they will agree, Unico will commit to hiring their top graduates."

"Wow," Johnny cannot hold his excitement. "That will give our university national acclaim."

"Yes," Don says. "Especially when Unico will donate handsomely so that your university can get the biggest bang for their valuable education. And, Johnny, the person to talk to is not just the dean. When we deal on such a scale, I'll have to talk with the president. Is he a strong person?"

"You may say she is." Johnny grins to himself.

Chapter 24

Today is the last session I'm giving this academic year, and I'm going to break a tradition. Usually when I reach the end of the year I run out of steam, or even worse, I run out of interesting material. But not this time. This session we are going to cover the solution to the problem that has been haunting me for weeks. It's going to be a very special session. I even invited Johnny.

"Mark, will you please describe your environment to the class?"

Mark stands up and starts to fill the room with his deep voice. "As you know, we are no longer dealing with the A226. That modem is past history for us."

"It's current reality for our company." Ruth doesn't want anybody to misinterpret. "It's the biggest success we ever had."

"True," Mark smiles proudly at her. "Anyway, the three of us are charged with the task of shrinking the development time of . . . all development at Genemodem."

"Yahoo," Ted whispers.

"Right from the start we knew that the biggest challenge

would be to deal with resource contention." Mark pauses to find the proper way to explain the essence of their challenge.

"Haven't we already dealt with that?" Roger asks. "I thought that resource contention was solved by the concept of critical chain. What am I missing?"

If somebody has gone through a paradigm shift, it's Roger. He's dropped his facade of 'I know it all,' and developed a keen interest in the subject. From time to time he even seeks my help on implementation issues. That shouldn't be mistaken for a change in personality. He is still as cynical and self-centered as he was.

"Critical chain," Mark explains, "removes resource contention within a project. It does not address resource contention between projects at all."

"Why don't you use the same logic for a bunch of projects? What's the difference?" Ted doesn't see the conceptual difference between one project and many.

Before Mark is able to answer, I interrupt. "Ted, in your company you do work on more than one project at a time."

"Of course."

"So you must have enough intuition to answer your own question. Try. Give an educated guess. What might be the problems?"

"Offhand, I see a synchronization problem."

"Synchronization is an impressive word," I say. "So impressive that it's often used to disguise ignorance. Ted, you don't want us to suspect you of such a thing."

"No way." And he jumps to the other extreme. "Resource contention means that the same resource is supposed to do two different steps at the same time," he wastes our time defining a term that is clear to us. "Removing resource contention between two steps," he continues methodically, "necessitates, many times, postponing one of those steps. The problem is that, as we discussed at length, there is no clear way to decide which step to postpone. It is almost an arbitrary decision."

I like the way he's approaching it. In order to force him to continue, I prod, "The same is true within one project. Why is it a bigger problem when the steps belong to two different projects?"

"Because two project leaders are involved," he confidently answers. "It's not like you work in one domain, where it doesn't matter which step you move. Here each project leader will naturally fight that the step to be postponed will not be his."

"Is it a big problem?" I continue my almost rhetorical questioning.

"Are you kidding?" Ted smiles. "Mark, now I see what you are facing. It's not just a synchronization problem, it's a nightmare."

"Fair description," Mark agrees. "Unfortunately we didn't realize how big the nightmare was before we stepped into it."

"With both feet," Ruth adds.

"Not because we are thick," Fred hurries to put in a caveat. "But because we didn't know what else to do."

"Do you want to hear what happened?" Mark asks.

I'm not the only one asking rhetorical questions.

"Well, the first problem was mechanical. Our projects, like almost any sizable projects, are described by about one hundred steps. You know, it takes some time to play with one hundred pieces of paper until all resource contentions are resolved. You move one piece to remove contention with one resource, and you have to move the other steps on the same path. This, many times, creates contention for other resources. It takes hours. Now, imagine doing it with six projects."

"So," Fred continues, "we went to our computer department."

"And that's the end of the story," Brian interrupts. "In my company everything you ask from the computer department takes months.

"It's the same in our company," Fred replies. "But we pulled rank. You see, our task is regarded as super, ultra, top priority. So we got a 'good-enough' piece of software from them pretty quickly. We loaded all the data, and then we started to play."

"And play. And play." Ruth laughs.

"These computers are an excellent way to procrastinate," Mark agrees. "We were dealing with minute contentions, things that if we had to do them manually, we would never have bothered. But we removed all contentions. Then, of course, as Ted predicted, we had to fight with all the project leaders."

"To cut a long story short, we squeezed agreement," Fred summarizes days of fierce arguments into one sentence.

"Then reality showed us what fools we were. Any speculations on what happened?" Mark asks the class.

Everybody is thinking hard, but nobody comes up with any ideas. Not even Ted.

Mark doesn't wait long. "Did you ever see a step that finished somewhat late?" He gives them a clue. "One small deviation in one step and BOOM—you get the domino effect, contentions all over the place. We found ourselves wasting all our time sorting out fights. Ted, you called it a nightmare? You are absolutely right."

"I can see it clearly," Ted agrees. "It could easily happen in my place. So what did you do?"

"Before we see the solution," I say, "can you tell us the conceptual mistake you made?"

"We were treating estimates as if they were real," Ruth answers.

"What do you mean?" I prod.

"Suppose a step was supposed to take ten days. You know there is a good chance it might take seven or fifteen, but we fed ten days into the computer. Then we treated this number as holy."

"I still don't understand," I say.

"We regarded contentions of three days as significant even when the estimate for the path was thirty days."

"Basically," Fred clarifies further, "we fell into the trap of thinking that eight times eight equals exactly sixty-four; we were trying to be more precise than the noise. Everybody was fighting about contentions which, left alone, could have been easily absorbed by the buffers."

"As a result," Mark summarizes, "we were constantly changing schedules for nothing, and by that creating real problems."

"I understand," Brian says. "And thanks for telling us about it. Now I know what not to do myself, but I don't know what to do. We cannot ignore contentions.

"Absolutely," Mark agrees. "We cannot ignore contentions in one project, we definitely can't ignore them when we look at all projects."

"You see the dilemma we were caught in? Fred asks. On the one hand, we had to consider contentions, but on the other hand, when we did, we ran into the nightmare."

"So what did you do?" Brian is eager to find the answer.

"We called Professor Silver in to help."

"Which was totally unnecessary," I emphasize. "You knew the answer. You were just too lazy to realize it."

"That's unfair!" Ruth rebels. "Even after you showed us, it took me some time to digest."

"The answer was taught to you by Professor Fisher in your production course, and then it was elaborated on by Professor Wilson in your systems course."

I know that I'm unfair. I spent weeks working on it myself before I figured it out. But I want to open my students' minds to the possibility of transferring a good concept from one field to another.

"We are dealing here with resource contention problems," I start to explain. "Have you seen the same problem in your production course?"

"Of course," Brian says. "Every time there is a queue of tasks in front of a machine and the priorities are unclear, we have resource contention; a few tasks are fighting to be processed at the same time by the same resource."

"Exactly," I say. "And how do you handle such a case? You have learned that it is foolish to try to schedule the work of each and every machine. What are you supposed to do?"

"Identify the bottleneck," Charlie says.

"And then?"

"Then exploit it; schedule the sequence of work for the bottleneck."

"By that," I say, "you have eliminated any contention on the constraint. You don't ask it to do two things at the same time. And then? Charlie?"

"And then subordinate. Subordinate all the other resources to it."

"And what is the result?" I ask. I am getting good at asking rhetorical questions. Rhetorical to these students who have learned it from Johnny.

"By that," Charlie replies, "you have removed most of the overloads from the other resources. And the sporadic peaks of load that still exist can be absorbed by the buffers."

"Exactly," I say triumphantly. "Why don't we do the same in projects?"

"But in projects we don't have a bottleneck," Ted reacts too quickly.

"Really?" Mark asks ironically. "In your company you don't have a bottleneck? Remember, we are not talking about one project; we are talking about all of them together."

"I see."

"And what is the impact of not acknowledging such a bottleneck?" I ask. "It's not just that it creates havoc synchronizing between the projects. You will get the same devastating impact we get in production. Not paying special attention to the bottleneck, not protecting it from Murphy with buffers, unavoidably results in wasting time on the bottleneck."

"Which causes," Fred continues, "a reduction in the overall throughput of the organization. We deliver fewer projects in total than we could."

"So," Mark takes over, "we identified the bottleneck. Very easy, we knew it all along. It is our digital processing department. And then we scheduled their work."

"How?" Brian interrupts.

"The same way we do it in production. There the priority is mainly determined by the due dates of the orders. In our case, by the targeted completion dates of the projects."

Ruth continues, "And from there it was easy. We went back to dealing with each project as a stand-alone. The impact of the other projects was taken into account by the additional information we got from scheduling the digital processing department."

This explanation is too abbreviated for most.

"In every project we have steps done by digital processing," Fred elaborates. "The schedule of the digital processing gave specific start and finish dates for these steps. So, for each project we first did the work as if no other project existed. You know, removing any major contentions. Then we adjusted the project to fit the digital processing dictates."

"Did it change the critical chain?" Ted asks.

"For some projects it did," Fred acknowledges.

"Then you put in the buffers?" Brian checks.

"Of course," Mark answers. "But here comes a major point. All the buffers that we've talked about so far, project buffer, feeding buffers and resource buffers, are all protecting the individual project. Here we have to remember to also protect the bottleneck, the overall performance of our organization."

Ruth continues. "So we had to insert another buffer, the bottleneck-buffer. It's not as big a deal as it sounds. We decided that two weeks is more than enough, for us it is, and every path that goes through digital processing we schedule to start two weeks earlier. It's as simple as that."

The class is quiet. Everyone is trying to digest what they've heard. I don't break the silence.

"We are still not sure if scheduling just the digital processing department is enough," Fred says. "Remember, in production there is the need to sometimes consider not just the bottleneck but another capacity constraint resource, or two."

"How are you going to know?" Charlie inquires.

"We monitor the feeding buffers with hawk eyes, for early

warnings," Fred answers. "If a resource contention starts to exhaust one feeding buffer after another, we'll know."

"But only then will we declare it as another resource constraint, not a minute before," Mark is fast to interject. "We are not going to be hysterical and consider every department a constraint just because they claim to be overloaded. We've learned our lesson. Never again are we going back to that nightmare."

We are sitting in a small deli in New York eating breakfast. Me and my Judith. When in Rome act like a Roman, so I've ordered a bagel with cream cheese and lox. Not bad.

New York is Judith's favorite hunting ground. She has perfected it to a science. We don't wander from shop to shop looking for something that will catch our eye. Oh, no, we are much more sophisticated. Judith plans it all in advance, down to the specific shops and the best routes.

Yesterday we were after an Oriental rug. After seven shops I was too exhausted to continue counting. At six o'clock we went back to the second place we visited in the morning and the battle started. Half an hour later, nine hundred and forty dollars poorer, we stepped out, the proud owners of a small, staggeringly beautiful, Persian rug. "We saved at least four hundred dollars," Judith summarized the day.

"What is our target today?" I ask my general.

"An antique coffee service."

"I thought you were pleased with the china you got last year?" I like it, even though I must admit that at the time I didn't like finding out we were another five hundred in the hole. I even made a small fuss.

"Our china is fine. But we need a silver set. For special occasions," and casually she adds, "you have cheese on your chin."

I almost choke. Special occasions, like twice a year when the queen of England pays us a visit.

"Wipe your chin," she reminds me.

I do. "What's the budget?" I dare to ask.

"No more than six thousand," she answers. "It won't be easy, so this time you'll have to play your role when I'm bargaining. Don't just stand there like a depressed log."

Now that I have tenure we don't have to worry about saving for old age; the university pension will take care of that. But six thousand dollars? And for something that we'll never use? Then I see her point. It's a good idea.

Satisfied, I announce, "We are starting a collection."

"The Silver collection," Judith titles it.

I devour what's left of the bagels, and wave for a refill. "Over the years we'll build a collection that will be something." Jokingly I add, "Then we'll leave it to the town and people from all over will come to see it."

"I wish we could leave it to our kids," she says in a low voice.

"So do I. So do I."

Absentmindedly I drink my coffee. "I wish there was something we could do." I put the cup back. "Come on, Judith, let's conquer the city." I stand up, all ready to go.

"There is something," she says.

I move behind her to pull her chair back.

She doesn't stand up. "There is a way we can have a child."

I sit down again. "But, darling, I thought you were not willing to adopt?"

She puts her hand on mine. "There is a way to have our own children."

"But . . ." I feel weak.

She strokes my arm. "Nothing is wrong with my eggs or with your sperm."

"You mean a surrogate mother?"

"Yes."

I try to digest. We can have a baby.

"Rick . . . darling . . . let's go." She stands up. "It's out of our reach."

"No." I grab her hand and pull her back. "You're sure it's feasible? I know that in this thing nothing is guaranteed, but is it feasible?"

Standing, she replies, "Yes. But what's the point in torturing ourselves. We'll never be able to afford it. Let's go, honey."

"Are you willing to go through all it takes?"

"You know I am." She sits down.

"And if at the end we fail. Can you take it?"

"I'll still have you."

"Judith, if you are ready, I'll find the money. Whatever we need."

"There is one problem," she says.

"What?"

"We'll have to postpone the start of our silver collection. Is that okay with you?"

If it wasn't New York, we would probably be arrested for making a scene in public.

Chapter 25

They started early. By eleven, Rick had finished his presentation. There was no doubt that Don Pederson was impressed. He even said that this know-how will be of great value to UniCo.

Then Jim took the lead, and gave a presentation on the design of a computer system for project management. His presentation centered around the think tank's warnings about the ease with which a too sophisticated system can throw project teams into a nightmare. When he finished, Don did not hold back his praise.

They didn't go out for lunch. Johnny arranged for sandwiches.

Don is not entirely pleased. What he heard this morning dealt with only one aspect of projects. An important aspect, but not the most important one. In Don's opinion the most costly mistakes are made before the execution starts. They are made in the decisions; the decisions about which project to choose, the decisions defining the scope of a project. What he heard this morning was good, exceptionally good. But everything presented was geared to the work of the levels from the project leader down. What about helping the decision process of top managers?

He hesitates. He thinks about how to bring it up, if at all. These people have done an exceptional job, and he doesn't want to say anything that will be interpreted as criticism.

Besides, he already found what he wanted. This group can be trusted to develop new know-how. It would be nice if they were not restricted to just the logistical arena, if they were capable of covering also the financial aspects. Nice, but not mandatory. He decides to raise the issue of investment justification, but if they try to defend conventional methods, he is going to drop it.

"I'm going to spend the rest of the week with the team putting up our new facility here. I certainly can and will use what you have taught me," Don prepares the stage. "Let me ask your advice. Knowing project team leaders, they are going to ask for additional investments."

"Without a doubt," Rick agrees.

"Suppose they ask me for an additional ten million dollars for something that will help us start operations three months earlier. How should I evaluate it?"

"I'm sure that by adopting what we've talked about you can cut more than three months, without any additional investments," Rick says confidently.

"You are probably right," Charlene agrees, "but the question still holds. Suppose that an additional investment can bring forward the completion time of a project, how does one go about evaluating whether or not to invest?"

Don nods. Charlene, being a financial professor, is familiar with this problem, but he doesn't expect much. He has been involved in numerous discussions about investment justification, and nothing came out of them. As a matter of fact, he sometimes found himself frustrated by the inability of financial experts to recognize why he is not satisfied with the conventional methods.

"Why not judge by a payback calculation?" Rick asks.

Don is preparing to answer when, to his surprise, Charlene does. And she hits the nail right on the head. "Payback calculations do not properly take into account the most important factor, the scarcity of money."

Rick is puzzled. So are Jim and Johnny. Don just smiles to himself, waiting for Charlene to continue.

Charlene, being a good teacher, first clarifies the problem. "Rick, when do we face the problem of choosing between two projects? If one of the two alternatives, or both, don't eventually bring more than the investment there is no problem making a decision. So the difficulty is choosing between two good alternatives."

"Correct."

"Now, if both alternatives are good, why do we have to choose? Why not do them both? You see, the need to choose arises only when availability of money is a constraint."

Don is pleased with Charlene's clean explanation. He leans back in his chair waiting to hear more.

"Back to payback period," Charlene continues. "Rick, suppose that you face two alternatives. Both will give you two years' payback, but one requires an investment of one million dollars and the other ten million. Judging by the payback period, these two alternatives look the same, one is no better than the other. But when money availability is the constraint we know that the two alternatives are vastly different."

"For me they aren't," Rick jokes. "One million dollars is out of my reach to the same extent that ten million is." And then, without a smile, he adds, "And I think that for a conglomerate like UniCo, it also doesn't make any difference. One million or ten million does not represent any problem in terms of money availability."

"It does," Don corrects him. "We always have more investment opportunities than available money. Charlene, would you recommend using net-present-value as a criteria?"

"No," she answers. "It is a more sophisticated method, but I'm afraid that it's conceptually wrong."

Don straightens in his chair. That is also his opinion, but up until now, every financial expert tried to persuade them that net-present-value was the only prudent way to justify invest-ments.

"Net-present-value is the way to translate future investments and income into terms of current money," Don repeats the argu-ments he's heard so many times. "This method takes into ac-count that interest and inflation exist; that one hundred dollars invested or earned next year are not equal to one hundred dol-lars invested or earned today. What's wrong with it?"

"You just said it," Charlene answers. "To estimate the value of investment this method uses interest, but we just said that as long as availability of money is a constraint, interest is not the appropriate measure."

"But isn't that what interest is all about." Rick doesn't under-stand. "If the bank charges me ten percent interest per year, isn't that the price I have to pay for holding the money?"

"Rick, go to the bank, offer to pay them, not ten percent, but twenty. Will they lend you a hundred thousand dollars?"

"Not without collateral," Rick admits, not revealing that is exactly what happened to him yesterday. Before Judith finishes the medical procedures, he may need more than one hundred thousand. Where can he possibly get it?

"You see," Charlene concludes. "The availability of money, which is at the heart of Don's question, has little to do with interest."

"Agreed," says Don. "We at UniCo are not pleased with ei-ther payback or net-present-value methods." With little hope, he asks, "Do you have a better alternative?"

"I think so," Charlene answers. "But I'm afraid you won't like it."

"Why not?"

"Because it necessitates developing new intuition."

Everybody waits for her to explain.

"We've just agreed that the availability of money is key for judging between investment alternatives. It is not difficult to prove that time is as important. If time were not part of the equation, if the return were immediate, we would not face any problem. We would invest in one alternative, get the immediate payback, and then invest in the other. We are dealing here with a two-dimensional problem, time and money."

"That's obvious," Don says.

"It is," Charlene agrees, "but we think in terms of time or money. We are not used to thinking in terms of time-money. Look at the methods we just rejected. Payback period is trying to give the answer in terms of time—two-years, three-years payback. Net-present-value is trying to give the answer in terms of money, of dollars. I'm afraid that the answer can only be expressed in terms of time and money, together, not separate."

"I don't understand," Don says.

"Let me give you an example from another field. There are things in reality that are very important. Nevertheless, since they involve summation of multiplications of two different dimensions, we have a hard time understanding them."

"I definitely have a hard time," Johnny interrupts. "Can you repeat that please?"

"Physicists know that one of the most important rules is conservation of momentum. They know that the summation of the masses of all the parts in a system, each multiplied by their corresponding velocity, is conserved, no matter what happens inside the system. Still, people outside physics have a hard time understanding this concept."

"I'm afraid that doesn't help me much," Don grins. "Can you give us a simpler example?"

"Suppose you have a field scattered with rocks. Do you agree that it is interesting to know the effort required to clean the field?"

"For some people . . ."

"How can we evaluate the efforts? We have to know the weight of each rock and the distance of each rock from the nearest border of the field. The effort to remove one rock is represented by multiplying the weight of the rock times the distance to the nearest border. Something we don't have a name for. The effort to clean the entire field is the summation of those multiplications.

"You see, here we have an example of something that can be presented only through a summation of the multiplications between two different dimensions."

"I see," says Don. "And I even vaguely see how it can be tied to the subject of investments. But can you please do it for us."

"Suppose you invest two dollars," Charlene prefers to explain in tiny steps. "After one day, you are invested for two dollar-days. After five days you are invested for ten dollar-days. Does this multiplication of money-time make sense to you?" She is ready to drop the issue in case of a negative response.

"Perfect sense," Don answers. "Please, continue."

"Now suppose that at the beginning of day eleven you invest another three dollars. For how much are you invested at the end of the day?"

"Let me see," Don tries to decipher. "My original two dollars are invested for eleven days, that gives us twenty-two dollar-days. On top of it I invested three more dollars for a day, which means another three dollar-days. In total I'm invested for twenty-five dollar-days. You are right, it is a summation of multiplications. But what's the point?"

"The point becomes clear when I tell you that on the morning of day twelve you got your five dollars paid back. Assume no inflation or interest. Are you satisfied?"

"No, I'm not," Don smiles. "I tied up my money for a period of time, I got back my money, but I didn't get any value for the fact that the money was tied up."

"Exactly." Charlene talks to him as if he is one of her students. "You invested twenty-five dollar-days. You got back your five dollars, but you are still twenty-five dollar-days in the hole. As long as this investment is not returned, you rightfully are not satisfied."

"I got my money back and I'm still in the hole?" Don doesn't get it at first.

They all think about it. "You are right," Don says after

awhile. "My investment is actually the summation of dollar-days. By the way, do you have a name for it?"

"I call it 'flush,' " Charlene almost giggles. "To be satisfied, you must make sure that you at least flushed out your investment. I stress it because at the end of the payback period, when everybody tells you to be satisfied that you got your money back, that's exactly the point in time that you are invested the most, when you are the deepest in the hole in terms of dollar-days."

"Now I also understand your warning about not having the intuition," Don says. "We regard money and investments as almost synonymous, but now I see how vastly different they are. They don't even have the same unit of measure. Money is measured in dollars, investment in dollar-days. I have to think about it, it may change our entire investment program."

He looks at his watch. "It's a pity I have to leave now, but I'm sure we'll have many more fruitful discussions. Johnny, can you please show me the way to your president's office? By the way, what does B.J. stand for?"

Eliyahu M. Goldratt's fascinating work as an author, educator and business pioneer has resulted in the promulgation of TOC into many facets of society and has transformed management thinking throughout the world. He has developed a powerful 8-session educational series that provides a common-sense approach to business that enables any organization to achieve optimal global performance.

For more information on Eli Goldratt and his current projects visit: www.eligoldratt.com

For information on other TOC books please visit our web site: www.northriverpress.com

Q